D0003897

A TASTE OF THE SWEET APPLE

A MEMOIR
Jo Anna
Holt Watson

A Taste of the Sweet Apple

Sarabande Books

LOUISVILLE, KENTUCKY

No part of this book may be reproduced without written permission of the publisher. Please direct inquiries to:

> Managing Editor
> Sarabande Books, Inc.
> 2234 Dundee Road, Suite 200
> Louisville, KY 40205

LIBRARY OF CONGRESS CATALOGING-IN-PUBLICATION DATA

Holt Watson, Jo Anna, 1935–
    A taste of the sweet apple : a memoir / by Jo Anna "Pee-Wee" Holt Watson.— 1st ed.
       p.   cm.
    ISBN 1-932511-08-3 (pbk. : alk. paper)
    1. Holt-Watson, Jo Anna, 1935—-Childhood and youth. 2. Woodford County (Ky.)—Biography. I. Title.
    CT275.H645533A3 2004
    976.9'465043'092—dc22   2003027684

Cover painting by Toss Chandler. Used by permission of the artist.

Cover and text design by Charles Casey Martin

Printed in Canada

This book is printed on acid-free paper.

A Taste of the Sweet Apple is the inaugural title of the
Woodford Reserve Series in Kentucky Literature.

This project is supported in part by an award from the National Endowment for the Arts. Funding has also been provided by The Kentucky Arts Council, a state agency in the Education, Arts and Humanities Cabinet, with support from the National Endowment for the Arts.

Sarabande Books is a nonprofit literary organization.

This is a literary work, not an historical document. Names have been changed. Liberties have been taken with the facts and characterizations, in the service of voice and narrative which are subject to imagination.

FIRST EDITION

For Joe Collins

Here is the place where Loveliness keeps house,
Between the river and the wooded hills . . .
Here you may meet with Beauty. Here she sits
Gazing upon the moon, or all the day
Tuning a wood-thrush flute, remote, unseen:
Or when the storm is out, it is she who flits
From rock to rock, a form of flying spray,
Shouting, beneath the leaves' tumultuous green.

Madison Cawein
1867–1914

Prologue

MY NAME IS ANNA, for the grandmother I never knew, but Joe Collins called me Pig. I was born after the time of my firebrand granddaddy, Richard Moses Harriss Holt, and, thankfully, before the time of television. I believe the countrified life my family led in those days gave us the gift of storytelling. Joe Collins and all the women in my family could spin a good tale.

My Aunt Sudie Louisa toted her tales from bridge table to fern-filled porches on summer afternoons, and whispered them over a cup of tea in wintertime beside the open fire. I sat at her feet as she narrowed her cornflower-blue eyes into tight little slits and spoke in a hush. My mother, Sallie Gay, could describe a room right down to the last detail, put you in it, close the door, and hold you there long after the story ended. Joe Collins held court by the ice-cold artesian spring in the middle of the day with the hired men, George "Double Yoke" Combs, Daddy Rat Parrish, and Will Middleton, who wore a patch over his right eye-socket like our mule Kate. She had a bad eye, too, and green flies were always at it. I suspected flies and gnats were pinned under his patch, too, but Joe said, "Best not to mention that." Daddy Rat was last to lumber down the hill; he was last at most everything. He bided his time until he could rest by the spring and eat Eva Belle Twyman's fried chicken and fried peach pies covered with a blue-and-white-striped tea towel. Eva Belle's hand could be found everywhere, even in the field beside the spring, inside a battered lunch pail. The men kept the spring water in a five-gallon metal bucket and we drank from a ladle with a long wooden handle.

Joe told the same old tales but they grew a little bigger and better each time. He rolled back his eyes until they were blind white hollows and drew up his fists to his face like a frightened child. Caught up in his spell, the men put down their dinner and something unseen doused us with cold spring water. He described gypsy caravans silently prowling the dark lanes through a heavy mist to form a circle on the very spot where we ate. Joe swore there was a troubled soul who appeared beside those who walked our Grassy Springs Pike on moonless nights. Dressed in her long white gown, she sighed and moaned as she floated among the old trees scarred by summer lightning. I believed completely. I looked for gold gypsy earrings in clods of dirt and saw dark-eyed gypsy women in the shadows of abandoned tobacco-stripping rooms. I loved Joe Collins' stories and they flowed from him like the clear water that poured from my granddaddy's ice-cold artesian spring.

My people have farmed the land in Woodford County since before the time of the Civil War. In 1942, when I was almost seven years old, we held about one thousand acres of land on Grassy Springs Pike, on McCracken Pike near the Glen's Creek, and on the Clifton Pike that runs straight down to the narrow, green Kentucky River. Joe always said, "Pig, our Grassy Springs Farm sits smack in the middle of the Bluegrass." We raised Southdown sheep, Angus cattle, and burley tobacco. Each generation of us attempted to breed a few fine horses. We claimed the rich limestone soil was the Fertile Crescent and the Land o' Goshen all rolled into one, and we called it "Heaven's Little Footstool," home to the world's finest burley, birthplace of premium bourbon and thoroughbred horseflesh.

Our Grassy Springs Farm was a few miles from the Keeneland racecourse and the sleepy town of Versailles, population 2,250 residents. The skinny telephone book listed two beauty shops, Ginny Rae's and Razor's, two banks, a blacksmith's shop, and several attorneys. My father, Doc, was one of three physicians. His office telephone number was 2, our home phone was 428, the C & D Grocery claimed number 1, and McCauley Brothers Feed Company 4. Only one veterinarian and one horse farm were listed.

Back in 1942, Buick introduced fluid drive, the clutch disappeared, and my mother, Sallie Gay, was greatly relieved; she never really understood the clutch and rarely used one. She dressed in her starched gray Red Cross uniform and ran the Hospital Women's Auxiliary in the basement of the Elementary School, served on the Altar Guild—and faithfully—played duplicate bridge at least two days each week. In those days, ladies wore gloves, girdles, nylon stockings with seams running up the back of the leg, and hats with veils as gauzy and delicate as spider webs. Gentlemen as well as children stood when those ladies entered the room; and uniformed elevator boys wearing white cotton gloves nodded politely and said, "Good afternoon, Madam." In the summer we slept under oscillating electric fans out on the sleeping porch upstairs and were none the worse for it.

When the Japanese attacked Pearl Harbor the morning of December 7th, America went to war. Congress officially adopted "The Pledge of Allegiance" six months later on June 22, 1942. Old Glory's stars-and-stripes flew in every city and town across the land, even on magazine covers: The Walt Disney comics I bought for ten cents featured Donald Duck and Pluto in US Army helmets, carrying the American flag; *Poultry Tribute* showed a child of seven saluting *eggs with flags;* Jimmy Cagney paraded across *Screenland Movie* magazine singing "Yankee Doodle Dandy." Scout troops collected scrap metal, paper, and rubber for recycling. In the classrooms, children were taught the values of democracy, citizenship, and loyalty, as well as thrift and sacrifice. Racehorses were named "War Stamp" and "War Bond" and at the Keeneland track they bet the Victory Double.

Despite the war, my family lived an insular, bucolic life. Our tobacco crops flourished, Doc's medical practice thrived, and the bourbon flowed. My daddy was a highly opinionated man and, like my granddaddy, he challenged authority and spoke with a mighty roar when it came to politics. FDR led America into World War II without Doc's approval, so he ignored all mandatory rationing imposed upon gasoline and many other necessities. He installed his own gasoline pumps out behind the stable, lit up a dark Cuban cigar and crowed, "That'll get FDR's nanny!" He wrote scathing letters to the President, violently objecting to his policies at home and abroad, which ultimately brought a formal admonition from the government, advising him, in no uncertain terms, to cease his un-American activities. The notice pleased him no end and inspired him to continue his seditious letter writing with renewed dedication. When Keeneland opened a few years earlier in the bleak grip of the Great Depression without his approval, he barked, "The Hal Price Headly crowd should have asked *my* advice—that little track stuck out in the middle of nowhere will never make a dime." (But like the man who named his horse "Advice" so nobody would take him, nobody asked Doc's advice and Keeneland became world famous for thoroughbred racing and sales.)

But the quiet man who really oversaw our farmland and cared enough to hold my unpredictable, hot-blooded family together was Joe Collins. He could have managed tobacco crops in any of the five counties of the Bluegrass; he was offered the position of floor manager at the Grower's Tobacco Market over in Lexington, but he turned that down. He chose to live in a green cottage on our property and take his toddy with Doc most evenings while they stewed over dry spells, or the heavy rains they called "toad stranglers."

While Doc tended to his patients and attacked the President, Joe Collins tended to the land, the livestock, and ran a crew of eight hired men every day of every week. I rarely saw him idle yet he always found time for me, and through his eyes, I grew to know the soul-satisfying pleasure that comes from working the land, the mysterious smell of damp fertile soil in the springtime, and the endless seasons of tobacco. Joe Collins was not just my ally and my hero, he was my best friend. He believed in me, he gave me my first chew of tobacco, and he taught me to spit three feet, too.

As I passed from one phase of my life to another, I allowed all their voices to wax and wane. I hid the olden days out of sight in a treasure chest carved in dark exotic wood, smooth as silk and inlaid with ivory. I kept my granddaddy's now-worthless stock certificates sealed in a lock box at the bank, just in case our oil wells in Texas might blow and make us all billionaires. And then one day I gave in to the voices and slowed my life to a crawl. I set aside my travels and endless projects, sold my business, and even put away my tennis racquet, to seek a quiet place where I could go back home and listen to their "small talk." I expected the journey would be painstakingly slow, like meticulously skimming cream or peeling fragile layers of tissue-thin onionskin; instead, my people bolted out of the barn door, talking a blue streak!

Spicy sweet Apple Chewing Tobacco burned the tip of my tongue. I smelled bluegrass on the old mules' hot breath, and settled into Aunt Tott's white wicker rocking chair on her breezy porch festooned with colossal ferns. I rode down narrow lanes on the running board of my daddy's silver La Salle automobile, trudged across fields of bluegrass and red clover behind Joe Collins. Eva Belle Twyman kneaded her buttermilk biscuits while June apples sizzled in cast-iron skillets on the stove. My beautiful mother's mysterious sea-green eyes flashed with life again, and the longer I lingered there, the more my heart ached for those times forever gone.

There was a shade tree in my youth. I stood beneath it to gather the pale blush of ripe crabapples for Eva Belle's jelly, a clear salmon-pink like the color of my mother's Elizabeth Arden powders and lotions. Joe Collins stood under that tree to smoke his Lucky Strike cigarettes. We stood under it together to gather guinea hen feathers.

Late one summer evening, as I sat at my desk remembering the day Joe Collins and I hunted for the guinea feathers, I was startled to discover the depth of my longing to see again what was there for me so long ago. I sat between Joe Collins and fat Daddy Rat Parrish on the grassy banks of my granddaddy's ice-cold artesian spring, as Joe spun blood-curdling tales of sly gypsies who stole little children from their beds in the middle of the night.

Part One

The Pink Bandanna

JOE COLLINS STOOD WELL OVER six feet tall. He had a strong
back and powerful arms, yet he was a gentle man. Most farmers
wore overalls, but to me, the faded-blue Fink's Joe wore were made
especially for him. *"FINK'S OVERALLS WEAR LIKE A PIG'S
NOSE!"* a dancing piglet boasted on the label. Joe wore a white
undershirt beneath the overalls, a greasy tan Stetson on the back of
his dark round head, and, in the summertime, dusty ankle-boots
without socks. In his front left-hand pocket he kept a pack of Lucky
Strike cigarettes with a box of safety matches, while deep in the
other bib pocket sat a cake of the sweet Apple Chewing Tobacco
wrapped in bright red cellophane. Tucked into a side pocket hung
a bandanna handkerchief, long ago faded to a pale pink. The other

pockets held some change, a box of Sen-Sen for his breath, and the little penknife with a pearl handle that my granddaddy RM used on the day he pitched over stone-cold dead in the cucumber patch. A worn brown-leather wallet rode in his hip pocket, molded into a half-moon shape from driving ol' John Deere, the tobacco setter, the Grassy Springs farm truck, and my daddy's silver La Salle. "Bring it on, little Pig," he liked to boast. "Joe Collins can drive it!"

Joe Collins smelled like sweet Apple Chewing Tobacco and Lucky Strikes cigarettes. I smoked sometimes while I rode beside him in the truck, or out in the tack room where I kept *my* Luckies, butts, and a package of Roll-Your-Owns in one of Doc's fancy Cuban cigar boxes. Through the years, the weed's scent had soaked itself deep into the soft leather seat of our truck: it worked its way into every thread of our clothing, and dry shredded leaves were mashed beneath the battered black lunch pail I held between my ankle boots on the truck floor.

One pale blustery afternoon in the early spring, when snow flurries kicked up without warning and flakes melted before they hit the ground, I stood next to Joe Collins on a rise in the middle of a pasture and we ate ourselves some good, rich dirt. He said it was time we went into the fields to test the soil. "When the earth commences to hint of spring, little Pig," he always said, "I go to ground like a fox!" He smelled the dirt, tasted it, and it told him if time and place were right for his seedbeds. The Grassy Springs truck bumped slowly over the barren field of deep furrows until he spotted a place to his liking and pulled to a halt. We climbed down onto brittle bare earth still hard and full of winter through my boots, and as we trudged over the deep ruts and last year's tobacco-stalk stubble, I thought the earth might never thaw, much less make a good seedbed.

He stopped and began to work the dirt loose, first with his heel, then with the toe of his boot. I did the same with my heel and the toe of my boot. He knelt down slowly on one knee. I knelt. He gathered up a handful of the dark soil. I pulled off my wool mittens and took a handful. He brought the earth to his nose, closed his brown eyes, and breathed deeply. His brow was pinched right in the middle of his forehead. He looked like this when he sipped that first cup of Eva Belle's strong black coffee while breakfast steamed in our kitchen at six-thirty on a cold winter morning. "Strong enough to bear up an iron wedge, that coffee is *ready!*"

"You smell a little springtime in it, Pig?" He asked me, his eyes still shut tight. "I can smell it," I told him. "I can *taste* it, too." He looked down at my dirty face and chuckled, "I reckon you *can* taste it for a fact." My nose, my mouth, and my chin were smeared with mud, and grit ground between my teeth. He licked his forefinger and carefully tasted a pinch of soil, pulled the bandanna from his overalls pocket and dabbed at his mouth. "The land gets a good hold on you," he murmured. "I might as well be *married* to her." He worked a little dark earth carefully between his fingers, crooking the little one as if he held a delicate porcelain teacup. "You remember, when my time comes, to add Joe Collins to this earth; you see to it, Pig. You hear me?" I looked him squarely in the eye, "Yes, I will, yes, Sir."

But I knew he would never leave me. He stood up, brushed off the knee of his overalls and handed me his worn pink bandanna. "You clean your nose and your own mouth good." I wiped at my face as we started back to the truck, and then sly as that fox he talked about earlier, I slipped the bandanna into my coat pocket and shoved my mittens down hard on top of it. How long, oh Lord, how long had I dreamed of possessing that scrap of faded pink cotton cloth. It *was* Joe Collins.

That man was *never* without a bandanna hanging from a pocket of his Fink's, or tied round his forehead or his neck to catch the sweat in the middle of a hot humid Kentucky summer. When we rode on the old wooden sledge behind the mules, he spread the bandanna carefully over his head like a fine damask tablecloth and set his greasy felt hat with a wide brim over it and swore, "This is one scorcher of a day, Pig. It's hotter then the hinges of hell out here in this patch." One thing was for sure: I wanted that bandanna bad enough to steal it. I stuck my hand in my pocket on top of the mittens to bury it deeper.

He was still carrying on about the soil, about farming, being married to the land and being buried in it, and as we walked to the truck, he didn't notice. "You never got time on your hands when you work the land, I can tell you. It's all the time that something wants to be fixed or painted or planted or hauled or get itself born . . ." I didn't listen to him; I was bursting with the excitement of my thievery, but I felt sick having taken something, anything from Joe Collins. "You sit yourself here on the running board and take off your dirty boots," he told me;

then he stepped around to the other side, muttering, "A little more mud on the floorboard of this truck and we can plant a crop right here." He opened his door and hauled himself up onto the seat. "Good God amighty, little Pig, springtime can't come soon enough for these stiff knees. Doc's right when he says, 'If you want to dance you got to pay Mister Piper.'"

They were forever talking about Mister Piper, Mister Piper, Mister Piper. It seemed to me everybody owed Mister Piper *something*, even my mother and Eva Belle talked about paying him. Aunt Sudie Louisa narrowed her blue eyes and hissed, "A disgusting little pervert was arrested in the Lyric picture show Saturday morning. That's when the little children watch their cowboy pictures and don't tell me he didn't know it; *he'll* pay the Piper or my name's not Sudie Louisa Harriss Hunt Hall!" "Who is Mr. Piper?" I asked with a frown. Joe stopped and cocked his head to one side and looked at me with his brow drawn together again. "You know, now that you ax me, I have to say, I don't rightly know *who* that is." And then he raised his eyebrows with a new thought: "Most likely somebody down at the courthouse in the County Clerk's Office." He settled himself behind the steering wheel and turned the key; I pulled the pink bandanna from its hiding place and handed it over. "I wanted to keep it," I told him. He took the faded handkerchief from me and tucked it into his overalls where it belonged. "You got to pay Mister Piper, too, Pig." Then he cranked over the engine and winked at me.

As we rode home through a chilly light drizzle, he said, "Don't talk to me about Little Miss Spring; she takes her good sweet time." And then he mused, "First blossoms then a frost, blossoms then a frost. April's a fickle one alright, doesn't know her own mind." Joe Collins was right about that, too: foolish forsythia, our fresh harbinger of spring, never learns her harsh lesson. "She's hellbent-for-leather to be first out and she's first one nipped in the bud or my name's not Collins!" But my mother said forsythia was the brave one, suffering capricious April's frost, sacrificing her pale lemon blossoms as a warning to others so eager for springtime and new life, her wilted yellow blooms cautioning them to wait until the mischievous little snow showers slowly turned to rain, when we could hear the deep sullen rumble of thunder again.

On those unseasonably mild days, when even the rain was warm, I raced outside in my shorts and bare feet to slosh across the lawn, twirling and skipping, caught up in the spell of an afternoon shower and held in its balmy misty womb. Lightheaded with colors and smells and sounds, I watched spring come strutting on stage in full costume like a peacock, marching to the music of blossoms opening wide: blushing tulip magnolia, sprays of peppermint pink and white dogwood, dark secret redbud, purple crocus, and rainbows of pompous tulips unafraid of a late frost or of startling snow flurries that turn up too late for their own good. Jonquils, rich as churned butter, rush to spread themselves over roadsides, meadows, and lawns, and then politely step aside to make way for a sea of pristine white snowdrops and violets. There is a fairy-tale cast of palest lime on the pastures. New leaves and slender young shoots are a startling green like the praying mantis or infant budworms just hatched on the underside of Joe's tobacco leaves. Suddenly there is a pastel radiance to the sky, soft moist air, and the sweet fragrance of lavender and white lilac, when spring comes again to my Kentucky.

Joe Collins paid the mysterious Mister Piper alright: he carried a half-dozen pieces of birdshot in his right knee, and said he could move them around with his finger and count them underneath his overalls. Doc said he got just what he deserved for shooting doves in a baited field over in Midway. "By God, you're one lucky son of a gun. It's a wonder the game warden didn't trip right over you, hiding in a row of corn, nursing a knee shot full of lead." Doc offered to remove the shot but Joe liked to tell the tale about the day he got his limit and took some number-eight pellets in the knee while shooting doves with the Governor, the Mayor, two Circuit judges, and the undertaker. But later on, just as Doc warned, the knee was struck with a bad case of the *artheraetus,* as Joe called it. "That knee, he's not working today," he'd say. When he pulled himself up into the truck or lifted the heavy harness for the mules, he placed his hands on the small of his back and stretched and sighed. "Old man Arthur struck like a thief in the night, little Pig. My back's stiff as the ironing board down in Miss Ermine Grundy's laundry." Sometimes when he was down in the back, he put Little Rabbit Green or fat Daddy Rat Parrish on the tobacco setter and let *them* bounce all day long over a field full of deep furrows, a gunnysack on their laps piled high with young, green tobacco plants.

He had corns on his toes and a painful bunion; when he heard about fallen arches, he said, "I suspect I've got them, too." The bunion acted up occasionally and he commenced hobbling and rocking from side to side, so Eva Belle and I called him "Ferry Boat." Doc threatened to hogtie Joe long enough to put a good pair of socks on him. "You asked for every corn on those crooked toes of yours, wearing boots without socks, and I'll bet you have at least a dozen pair of good wool socks with the price tags still hanging on them." The price tags *were* still on the socks and the socks were piled underneath his bed along with neckties, gloves, wallets, and occasional pipes he received at Christmas. The possessions he treasured were laid out as neat as a pin on top of his *chester drawers:* a framed black-and-white photograph of a younger, thinner Joe Collins standing beside the new Grassy Springs farm truck, a half dozen twelve-gauge shotgun shells in bright red casings with brass trim stood shoulder to shoulder like toy soldiers, the little penknife with a pearl handle my granddaddy RM left him, a pack of Lucky Strikes, a box of safety matches, a pair of genuine leather brushes he never used on his hairless head, and some loose change in an ashtray from the Canary Cottage Restaurant. Joe said you could tell a lot about a person when his things are laid out in fine order like that.

I hid things away just like Joe did, but on the back shelf of my closet. I stashed my white ermine muff with its pitiful tail and feet there, after Joe said it looked like the little weasels that scampered in out of the cold to winter in our corncribs. I buried the infernal dotted-swiss blouses that gave me a red itchy rash under my armpits; I hid the stiff white patent-leather sandals that made my socks slip down to knot beneath my arch.

––––––

Doc once gave me a ten-dollar gold piece wrapped in white tissue paper inside a yellow envelope from the Woodford Bank and Trust Company. Sallie Gay and Aunt Sudie Louisa both told him, "She is *entirely* too young to have such a thing," but he said, "Pig knows how to take care of her money, she's Doc's little girl." I raced upstairs to squirrel away the treasure, stuffing the bank envelope in a pair of brand new filmy white socks with lace on the cuffs. I packed that into a stiff patent-leather sandal, and sealed the whole kit and caboodle inside a shoebox where I hid the jars of Vicks VapoRub. I hid Vicks from Thanksgiving until Easter, but they always found some more.

I stood on a chair and buried my gold coin in a dark corner on the top shelf where no one could ever find it. For all I knew, Joe might have a gold piece stuck inside a wool sock underneath that bed of his. I wasn't sure about that, but one thing was for sure, nobody but Joe Collins would ever know where I hid *my* ten-dollar piece of gold. It was my treasure, but far greater to me than money was his worn-out handkerchief. If I had found the nerve to keep his bandanna that raw gray afternoon in the tobacco patch, I would have buried it right along with the ermine in the darkest corner of my closet so I could sneak it out, tie it around my neck, and wear it in the pony barn as I ran the currycomb through manes and tails, or when I sat all alone in the tack room, thoughtfully working saddle soap into bridles and saddles, pretending I was Joe Collins, giving a little sigh now and then like he did, "Old man Arthur struck like a thief in the night..." I would sooner have given up my piece of gold than his washed-out scrap of pink cotton.

Old Man Tobacco

JOE COLLINS ALWAYS SAID, "Old man *Tobacco*, he rules the roost and he's a backbreaking, money-making crop!" Life limped along or cakewalked to the tune of Tobacco and it played inconsistent notes. In those days, burley tobacco was king and that crop set our life in the Bluegrass apart from the rest of the world, demanded we operate on a different calendar. Joe mothered every crop, every year like it was his long-awaited first child, and like every farmer who ever planted a seedbed, he fussed and worried from spring until Christmas over the weather, the destructive, hardly visible red aphids, and the plump green budworms that wanted to gnaw on the undersides of his plants. He worried too much rain would bring on Blue Mold, and then he worried there would not be *enough* rain. And would we catch a dread disease called Black Shank? Year in and year out, old man Tobacco determined the seasons of Joe Collins' life.

Farming was not just an occupation, but a way of life that colored our days from birth till death. Farm tasks are endless in spring as in every season; planting, cleaning and oiling harness, readying machinery, and putting in a sizable vegetable garden of tomatoes, peas, onions, peppers, beets, carrots, corn, melons, and herbs. Joe said, "We just can't wait to put in the garden, little Pig, so we can keep busy all summer praying and hoeing." In April, seedbeds are fertilized, sowed, rolled, and raked, *by hand*. The tiny seeds are mixed with more fertilizer, spread carefully over the soil, and then covered with straw and cotton, *by hand*. Joe Collins called them his nurseries, those long straight rows of seedlings protected with soft cloth. In May, thousands of tender young plants are pulled, *by hand*, and row after row of them carefully set, *by hand*, handled as delicately as sprays of fragile baby's breath from my mother's flower beds.

Joe said, "I'll tell the world, a tobacco setter is a magical piece of farm equipment. How does it know to scoop up a handful of dirt, and then wait just long enough for a plant to be dropped in between the sharp blades? How in this world and the next does it know to water the plant?" It takes four people to set tobacco, one to drive the tractor, two to drop the plugs, and one to walk along behind and act as the pigtail, picking up plants left on the ground and filling the gaps. The men rode the setter but Joe Collins never let me ride. I had to be the tagalong pigtail, but that's not why he named me Pig. He said he took to calling me that because I rooted and rummaged where I had no business. He said I loved trouble like a hog loves slop. On bright spring mornings, I tagged along right at his heels to watch the men roll the old setter out of the barn and oil it up to work another season behind John Deere. I nagged him to let me ride on it and set tobacco and, as it did most of the time, my ear-splitting caterwauling finally wore him down. He gave in and said I could sit across from his brother Zack to plant just one long row. He told Zack, "This child squeals like a litter of pigs if things don't go just right for her." He frowned at me and stuck out his lower lip, "If I let you ride the setter, don't you take one eye off your work, you hear me? Why, that razor-sharp blade would just as soon take your fingers and set them out alongside the plants."

He thought he could scare me off by looking ugly and carrying on about razor-sharp blades. He was trying to call my bluff so he wouldn't have to fool with me, but I was on to Joe Collins. He gave himself away every time he wagged his finger in my face and started that preaching business. Most of the time he had to laugh at himself, trying to sound harsh and look serious, so he turned his head away and spit some tobacco juice into the next row, then he dabbed at his mouth real slow with that pink bandanna so I couldn't see him grinning. Sometimes he just set his hands on his hips and took a good deep breath. He had my number alright, but I had that gentleman's number, too!

When I finally made it aboard that old red piece of machinery, I rode big as you please alongside Zack with a wet gunnysack of plants on my lap. Spring water in a fifty-gallon tank mounted on the setter sloshed back and forth—back and forth in time with the mules' slow gait—as John Deere's motor droned and hummed. It was as if all the bees in the world swarmed right over our heads that fresh morning in the tobacco patch. I never took my eyes off the sharp blades and I suspect I never took a good deep breath. Later, as we walked down to the spring with the hired men, Joe tilted his head to one side so the others couldn't listen in and he whispered to me, "Best not to mention the setter-riding to your mama or to Eva Belle either for that matter." "No, Sir. No, *Sir*," I told him, but he didn't need to caution me about that. The very thought of razor-sharp blades and gunnysacks would have brought on my mother's hot flashes to *who laid the rail*. We made ourselves comfortable on the grassy bank and I wiggled my bare feet in the water. "I swear, Pig," he muttered as he rummaged through his lunch pail, "I believe you set tobacco good as Zack." *Good as Zack! Good as Zack!* His seal of approval shot through me like bolts of summer lightning, heavenly hosts commenced to sing. "Yes, good as Zack," he said. Suddenly I was starved for Eva Belle's fried chicken, and blissful, sitting right beside Joe Collins, with my toes in granddaddy's ice-cold artesian spring. I was six years and ten months old, a farmer. I set my long row "good as Zack" and I still had all ten fingers. Joe Collins never said it out loud, but he was glad he let me ride that old setter. I could tell—like I said, I had that gentleman's number.

There's nothing new about inhaling smoke; the tobacco leaf has found itself in and out of favor over the centuries. In 3000 B.C.

Egyptians breathed frankincense and Romans inhaled burning rabbit fur and goat's horn to ward off something or other. The weed ran aground about 1600 when a Russian Czar declared tobacco a deadly sin, flogged offenders, and exiled them to Siberia—but later on it was lauded as a preventive of bubonic plague! Aztecs in South America and Mayas in Mexico smoked tobacco wrapped in palm leaves and corn husks, little Napoleon used seven pounds of snuff a month, American cowboys chewed tons of it ... but "seegars" outdid them all. By 1901, six billion cigars were sold in America alone. For over six hundred years, somewhere on the American continent, people have chewed, eaten, even rubbed tobacco on their bodies, and praised the weed as a remedy.

My people have raised prime burley tobacco on the Grassy Springs Pike in Woodford County since around 1850, and the sad truth is that it means nothing at all anymore: how meticulously seeds and fertilizers must be mixed and sown, how there are thousands of those tiny tobacco seeds in just one single ounce, the hand-pulling and setting of young plants, the weeding, topping, cutting, hanging, and stripping tons and tons of the broad golden leaves.

Varmint Stew

OLD MAN TOBACCO bound Joe Collins to the land and he would live out his days in the Commonwealth of Kentucky. He left just once to go only as far away as Nashville, Tennessee, with Doc and my Aunt Tott's dapper husband, Uncle Freddy McCammish, to pick up a worthless racehorse. Lord knows, there were plenty of us at home in his care, including sorrel mules, sheep, a herd of cattle, ponies, a half dozen other spirited mares and horses, his three brothers, his girlfriend Miss Mattie Combs, his good friend Ocean Frog, as well as Sallie Gay, Doc, and me. He fed the wild mallard ducks that lived on our pond, even a four-foot-tall blue heron that occasionally flew in to impress us. He looked after guinea fowl and peafowl roosting and screeching in the old crabapple tree, Doc's feisty little Bantam roosters, more than two dozen fat laying hens, and the whole lot of us showed up like clockwork day-in and day-out.

He saw to the automobiles and farm machinery. The fencerows were cleaned every spring, but hedgerows were left as a refuge for hares, squirrels, raccoons, and the occasional red fox. As soon as spring rains subsided he saw to it that the barns and gates were painted black, and that the smokehouse, henhouse, sheds, and two little cottages were given a new coat of dark green trimmed with black. A mile of irrigation pipe was laid in twenty-foot sections running from the lake on the back of the farm to the tobacco fields, and when that pipe was not in use, over three hundred units were stacked in one end of the hay barn, laid in close ranks like the fresh cigarettes in a brand new pack of our Lucky Strikes. Heavy harness and fine English tack were cleaned and saddle-soaped. Joe said he had a place for everything, and he saw to it that everything was in its place right down to the hams, shoulders, sides of bacon, and sausages. The hot sausages seasoned with hot peppers and sage were carefully wrapped in cheesecloth, and hung from the ceiling to hickory-smoke and age in the dimly lit smokehouse. How can I put into words the spicy perfume of sugar-cured hams in that close airless place? And there is no way to describe the sweet smell of a henhouse, a tack room, the corncrib, or a pigsty after a spring shower.

Late one afternoon, when it was warm enough to sit outside, I found him on the porch of his cottage, sewing buttons on his shirts. I took my seat on a three-legged stool next to him and began to poke around inside his sewing basket. Maybe it was his carefulness threading a needle, the pains he took with his mending, *woman's* work, that put him in mind to tell me that his mother died the very day he was born, leaving her baby and his three brothers behind: Ernest twelve, Zack four, and Dan only two years old. "I never did know her, not for one minute, and don't you know Ernest wondered what in this wide world he was going to do with me laying up in the kindling box, howling like a stuck pig. Ernest ran down the Pike to Miss Ada Mae Mundy for help and had it not been for her taking us in, we would have starved to death. She took every last one of us, raised us like her own, and called me Joe."

Ada Mae Mundy lived alone on her farm of twenty acres or so. She grew a truck garden and ran Mundy's Moving and Hauling, a two-pickup-truck operation and a very profitable business. She was an industrious woman, and as soon as the boys were able to use a hoe or carry a piece of furniture, she had them working the truck garden, loading and unloading the pickups, and cutting fire wood. Joe said, "I laid fires, tended the Jersey milk cow, and churned butter long before I could spell my name. Like you, Pig, I was crazy to drive anything I could get my hands on. I was steering Mundy's Moving trucks before I could see past the wheel."

He left the Mundy place the summer of 1904, when he was twelve, the last of the boys to go. Within a month my daddy and Joe Collins would meet. Right on the heels of his leaving, Ada Mae took two orphan girls and one boy under her wing, and she was never again without a clutch of children in her home and garden. And, you might know, Joe, his brothers, and her sizable brood of adopted children cared for her until her death when Joe was twenty years old. He said, "But for her taking us on, Pig, Joe Collins never in this world would have made it, at least a dozen of us children were better off knowing Miss Ada Mae." I knew Miss Mundy was better off, too, for knowing Joe.

He was informally engaged to be married to Miss Mattie Combs, and a photograph of her hung on the wall over his bed. I lived in mortal fear that one day he might marry her and move out to her fine house with its vegetable and flower gardens and the glorious spray of morning glories draped across her front porch. He saw to those gardens and painted her house spanking white every spring. He bragged that she was particular about everything around the house, and that was good news to me. I knew Joe Collins wouldn't put up with much of that *particular* business.

Joe was a man of the earth and he never met a stranger. He was at ease with the tobacco buyers from Reynolds Tobacco, American Tobacco, Brown and Williamson Tobacco, the United States Senator up the road, the Bridge Club, the Episcopal Bishop, and the walleyed laundress, Ermine Grundy, who went into strange reveries in the laundry. *HEY, yah, yah, HEY, yah, yah!* When she commenced her weird and wonderful chanting in the cool dark cellar, singing to the spirits, she stood frozen like a statue in the dim light, arms open wide, her head thrown back so far that her coal-black queue brushed her waist. Joe teased, "Lookout, Pig, Ermine Grundy's gone and got herself all trancied up again."

Joe was Honorary Mayor of Jacksontown, a settlement on the outskirts of the town (it's just possible he appointed himself), and he hosted an annual varmint supper for a dozen at Miss Mattie's out in the backyard. He cooked squirrel, rabbit, chickens, and groundhog with onions, potatoes, carrots, turnips, parsnips, and tomatoes, and the mess simmered all day long in a cast-iron pot until it was a dark, thick stew with inches of groundhog grease floating on top. He served it with hot corndodgers, slow-cooked kale greens, and cut the grease with Doc's bourbon. He called it a varmint supper and he bragged, "It's the loudest smelling stew in the county!" It was a big event and everybody talked about it for weeks, but no matter how much I begged, Joe Collins never once invited me to his supper. "May as well quit that racket," he told me, "I turn the deaf ear to your carrying on."

At dinner, when I asked Doc to say something to Joe about my going to eat the groundhog, he just laughed and shook his head. But Sallie Gay fell silent as a tomb. Slowly she brought her napkin to her mouth, held it there, and stared at me; my own mother gazed at me as if she had never seen me before. She looked like this when the down-and-out tramps pounded on the kitchen door looking for a handout, or when we came upon a possum squashed to a pulp in the middle of the Pike. "Lord have mercy upon us," she sighed. Another stalemate. Why were the things I loved best so strange, so distasteful to her? I wished I had never opened my mouth about that varmint supper. Sometimes, I talked too much.

By God, I'm Brilliant

WHEN MY FATHER ENTERED medical school the year was 1900, China was still ruled by The Empress Dowager, there were fewer than ten thousand automobiles worldwide, and Kodak introduced the Brownie camera for children. When he graduated four years later, Teddy Roosevelt was President of the United States, Ivan Pavlov was awarded the Nobel Prize for Medicine, and Vicks VapoRub permeated households across the nation. The common cold would never be the same again.

Doc rode the Louisville and Nashville Railroad home to find spring repair on the farm underway: buildings, fences, gates put right, hay balers and wagons oiled and greased, blades sharpened, tobacco plants already set in long straight rows, with my granddaddy RM right in the thick of the revival. Dressed in his high boots, a long tan duster, and armed with his walking stick, he directed carpenters and stonemasons. The fragrance of new grass and the potent familiar odor of loamy soil reclaimed the young doctor's heart and soul. New foals, calves, and snow-white lambs, RM's fine horses and sleek Angus cattle set his head reeling. He was home. In a few weeks he would celebrate his twenty-first birthday to officially become the man of his own dreams, Dr. Joseph P. Harriss Holt.

He was tall, slender, with blue-wildflower eyes and his light hair parted right down the middle. He looked more like an athletic teenage boy than a full-fledged physician, but there was little youthful whimsicality about *his* mercurial disposition. Doc was a spoiled, focused, intense young man who accomplished what-ever he set his quick mind to, and on the rare occasion when he did not have his own way—or, as a matter of fact, for no good reason at all—a dark brooding overtook him. He could throw a temper tantrum second to none. I wonder if he ever agonized over his quick-as-lightning mood swings, or did he take time to reckon with his hellion father's own fierce temper, and the heartache it caused my grandmother Anna? (His only sister, Aunt Sudie Louisa, proudly christened herself Hellcat, and she could throw a three-day fit if her long golden curls went limp or a blemish dared to mar her pretty pink cheek.)

Doc was granted the gift of healing, though. He knew this at twelve years old, when he performed abdominal surgery on a prized Hampshire sow that had gone mysteriously barren. My granddaddy gave orders to slaughter her, but fortunately for the old sow, the task was overlooked, giving the precocious boy the opportunity to prepare for surgery. With the aid of another child of twelve whose family lived and worked on the farm, the boy-surgeon and a spindly Eva Belle Twyman lured the sow, using ears of silver queen corn, into a penned area well behind the barn and far away from the house.

They laid her out cold with a rag soaked in chloroform and down she went like a ton. No one ever knew just how or where the child got his hands on a bottle of chloroform, but that's the way it came down to me. Eva Belle and Doc managed to roll her unwieldy mass over, to stretch her flat out on her back, and tie the sow to four stakes in the ground. They say he opened her up, removed a tumor the size of a cantaloupe, then stitched up his patient good as new—though admittedly sore as a boil. The sow would thrive. She bore healthy piglets within a year, the following year, and the next. I can see him now, narrowing those pale blue eyes and proudly showing his white, even teeth and thinking, "By God, I'm brilliant!"

Two years later, when he was fourteen, he was shipped off to The Miller School of Albemarle, a preparatory school where he excelled in every subject, became bored, and rigged the faculty four-hole privy with butter paddles to administer a keen slap in the bare behind the instant a teacher sat down. He was summarily expelled and sent back home to the farm. RM deemed the privy prank another stroke of genius on the part of his precocious son, petitioned the headmaster to reconsider, then crowed about teaching that school in Virginia a good lesson in creative uses of the butter paddle. "Paint life with a broad brush, by God, sometimes wrong, never in doubt!" he thundered. Joe Collins told me, "If old man RM had thought of it, he would have left instructions to carve those very words into his big white-marble tombstone out at the cemetery." The boy was allowed to return to school later. He behaved, or at least he was never caught again. He graduated, with honors, the youngest in his class, two months before his sixteenth birthday. He would ultimately be the youngest to graduate from The School of Medicine in the city of Louisville. There, paddle-wheelers festooned with gaslights slipped downstream at night, their calliopes broadcasting "I Dream of Jeannie with the Light Brown Hair" and "My Old Kentucky Home" over the Ohio. Barges loaded with Louisiana salt inched upriver, and foghorns wailed in the night. Sailboats and canoes skimmed and glided across her in fair weather, and he wondered if he could ever return to the farm.

As graduation approached he took stock of his future and his options. He considered further pursuit of his studies in the field of surgery, or he could easily settle into an accustomed life back home, where he would enjoy a full-blown practice of general medicine and surgery too, if he pleased. After all, who in the world would dare tell him not to wield his scalpel whenever he deemed it necessary? He saw himself as a big fish in that familiar little pond. He came home, took up residence in two front rooms upstairs in the New Woodford Hotel on Main Street, and rented office space three doors away in the old Minary Building across from the courthouse and the town bank. His return was celebrated by a few parties and by a piece in the "Dot Tell It All" weekly newspaper column. The "Tell It All" piece praised the young physician's good looks, ran on about his academic accomplishments, and advised young ladies to set their caps for the handsome doctor.

He counted the days until he was granted official license to practice medicine, arranging and rearranging his spotless office down to the last detail. He prepared bottles of violent red iodine, clear cool alcohol, ether, and his old friend chloroform, and lined them up in perfect order on new glass shelves. Gauze and strips of adhesive hung at the ready; polished metal hemostats, scalpels, scissors, clamps, and needles shimmered in a glistening new metal sterilizer: everything as spic-and-span and white as Miss Ermine Grundy's laundry room at the house, where an industrial-sized washing machine with soft white rubber rollers stood like an overweight matron on spindly legs in the middle of the concrete floor. In Doc's office, starched white sheets lay folded on his new metal examining table. Bright lights hung from the high ceiling and cast a clean white daylight onto the polished black-and-white tile floor, onto his black-leather medical bag and stethoscope, black microscope and the black-and-white set of scales standing against the stark white wall.

Across the room, beneath a large oval window that opened onto the street below, he set his mahogany partner's desk on a worn Moroccan rug. Over that he hung framed diplomas and degrees. A stack of pale blue prescription pads, the heavy black telephone, fountain pens, and books covered the desk, along with his class photograph. He bought red-leather furniture for his patients' comfort in the waiting room and my grandmother Anna placed heavy brass andirons in the fireplace. He found a good deal on a Lucas typewriter for Miss Lucy Hunter, who would be his receptionist and office manager until he was forced to retire.

One evening, after taking his supper late in the dining room of The New Woodford, Lady Fate played her trump card and sent Joe Collins to tap on his door: "My name is Joe Collins. I'm twelve years old," the small boy said. He asked if he could hire on, tend to the doctor's horse, do office chores, and stay with him. Well, hire on he did, and the two men forged a bond that spanned forty years until Doc went to his grave at sixty-two. From the very beginning, Joe Collins said, there was no stopping Doc. "Nobody stood in that man's path, Pig, not for love nor money."

Healing was Doc's heroic adventure and he practiced medicine for forty years with tender intimacy. I believe he longed all his life to be touched and held as he held the people in his care. He stood well over six feet and weighed two hundred pounds, wore a hat sized seven-and-a-half, and had a mane of blonde hair. Many times I saw him gently put his ear to a chest and listen to the beating heart, holding one hand carefully while he felt the pulse in the other wrist. He paid children under twelve a quarter when he vaccinated them, stuck a needle in the arm or the behind. When the sick could not afford his care, there was no charge, and if payment came later on, often it arrived on the back porch of our home in the form of fresh vegetables, preserves, bread-and-butter pickles, and even pieces of Sheraton or Chippendale furniture, usually painted a half-dozen coats of bilious green, seemingly a favorite color of the 1940s. I know for a fact it was never love of the almighty dollar that took him down that road.

A Yellow Dog Democrat!

————————————✐————————————

IN THE LATE SPRING, tiger-yellow Turk's-cap, yellow-fringed orchid, and her mysterious white monkshood opened up in the secret damp places down by the creek. As regular as clockwork, beds of violet-and-yellow Japanese iris appeared. My mother, Sallie Gay, looked to her flowers to find serenity. She played bridge, planned dinner parties, while Doc and my Uncle Freddy bet the races over at Keeneland, and Joe Collins and his crew hand-pulled the young tobacco plants, preparing to set out the crop right after Derby time in early May.

My mother was one of the prettiest women in the Bluegrass. Her Buck Pond Duplicate Bridge Club ladies took me by the chin, slowly turned my head from side to side, and heaved a sigh, "You certainly don't look like your mother, *do* you now." Sallie Gay wore her dark hair brushed up and away from her classic face and green eyes. In wintertime, she dressed in black with a string of pearls beneath fur coats that held a faint fragrance of cedar and Elizabeth Arden Blue Grass Cologne, or in her fitted gray wool dress trimmed at the neck and sleeves with Persian lamb and a hat to match. She loved hats—fur hats, tweed hats, hats with feathers or a turban for autumn, and elaborate candy straws with linen dresses in summer.

I loved it when she dressed in her Red Cross uniform, rolling bandages for the War at the Hospital Women's Auxiliary, or in a popular dress called a Golfer and an apron, working miracles in her cutting-garden of snapdragons, deep blue larkspur, and violet delphinium. Sprays and sprays of fragile white baby's breath, like lacy backdrops behind the flowers, grew along the old brick walks; pearl-white and pink peonies returned every year with blooms so heavy they hung their heads. One large brilliant bed was devoted to a shock of Oriental poppies and I could hear their bright red splashes of color. She was beauty and fragrance and the melody of those poppies.

I cherished every single minute we were together in the world of hoes, trowels, and rakes, mixing potting soil and manure, moving earthworms and fat grub worms with care. I can see her now, removing her straw hat and wiping her brow with the back of her wrist, flower-bed dirt on her apron and gloves, and there was even a smudge on her cheek. And I was happy to see her forehead was damp and the hair in ringlets around her face. We worked the moist spring soil until it was as fine as coffee, planting columbine, baby's breath, and more baby's breath; she loved baby's breath. I prized the times we worked all morning in her flowers, often until noontime when Kate Smith came over the radio belting out, *God bless America, land that I love,* down on our knees in the dirt, in my small world, working good rich cow manure into the earth.

I hung onto her every word, the way she used her hands when she told a story, tilted her head and smiled. I watched her move a chair a few inches and place a lamp or a bowl of flowers on the table by the front door, or pour over swatches of fabric and paint chips; I especially loved the looks of astonishment and admiration in the eyes of the bridge club ladies when she launched into an impromptu imitation of Greer Garson in *Mrs. Miniver,* the Academy Award-winning movie of 1942, or of Humphrey Bogart in *Casablanca.*

Everybody said she "had a way" with her. She arranged flowers in old copper urns and silver water pitchers. She liked the unexpected, used vegetables as centerpieces: bundles of fresh asparagus, celery, or carrots tied with ribbon in a terra-cotta flowerpot. She threw dramatic fabrics to the windows and on furniture, mixing bold stripes, polished-cotton prints, and on a large wingback chair, a Scottish tartan. She mixed period pieces with objects she came across in antique shops and auctions: a Scottish dagger, a collection of magnifying glasses, brass shields, and a leather trophy. She knew just where to place a portrait or mirror to catch the light. Her use of space ran outside to create the old brick walks that ran alongside her long curving banks of flowers. Dinner party tables were a production in damask, silver, crystal, and fresh-cut flowers. Sallie Gay had a good dose of style.

Her collection of music was eclectic. She purchased the stirring *Saber Dance* as soon as it was recorded in 1942, along with *Porgy and Bess* and *Rhapsody in Blue.* In the afternoon, after her nap, we listened to *The Magic Flute* and the London Orchestra's *Tales from Vienna Woods;* our lips quivered; we pretended to weep and swoon to *Madama Butterfly.* Sometimes, her dressing-table mirrors reflected the two of us holding hands, bathed in sunbeams, and swaying to *The Blue Danube Waltz.*

The details of managing the house were left to Eva Belle in the kitchen, Ermine Grundy, and Miss Sarah Hawkins who, Sallie Gay swore, tried to run the wheels off the Electrolux vacuum cleaner and polish the very hide off the furniture. The house operated like a well-oiled machine. Dinners and luncheon bridge parties appeared to be effortless, and sometimes my mother seemed to be a guest in her own home. Often, she stood alone on the long porch, making powerless judgments, and I knew, even then, serenity was a constant struggle amid Doc's chaotic mood swings that defied logic.

But identity was never a problem. She was an egalitarian, a yellow dog democrat and proud of it, a strong advocate of the President's New Deal despite Doc's loathing for FDR. "Don't talk to me about that piss ant," he growled. "He's a Fascist or a Communist, I don't know which one's worse, and he's the President of the United States, for God's sake. They say when they catch Herr Hitler he'll be sentenced to marry Eleanor Roosevelt, live in Indiana, and work at Belknap's Hardware Store! That's punishment enough for *anybody!*"

Sallie Gay considered the Republican Party a safe house for bigotry, and Eleanor Roosevelt the greatest woman of her time. "I have no time for Ellahnoah," Doc declared, "she's a Communist too. And just as sure as I'm sitting here, she's hellbent-for-leather to poison the mind of every colored in the country." They should have avoided the subject of politics on any level; the mere mention of FDR lit his fuse and she knew it. They were a whirling dervish of contradictions and maybe that's what bound them so passionately together and then blew them apart.

But sometimes our world was cool and pale, and their easy conversation so soft and muted it made the evening birdsong, crickets, and even the moan of doves sitting tight in the old trees, sound harsh. Our little world was oblivious to the earthshaking events occurring outside the Bluegrass. The times the three of us sat beside her flowers on warm spring evenings were some of the sweetest times we shared. Watching them and listening, I held the moment. They rested on soft mint-green cushions in white Adirondack chairs set close to her lemon lily beds and sipped tea with fresh mint. On the table, under the umbrella, a silver pitcher of ice water glistened and beaded and ran down to puddle on the tablecloth, where a small tray of chilled celery curls sat beside a crystal salt-dish.

Meanwhile, just up the road a piece, our neighbor, a United States Senator, cast the deciding vote to appropriate every red cent the President requested to produce the two atomic bombs America would drop in 1945. While we puzzled over names like Guadalcanal, Tarawa, and Bataan, my Aunt Tott patted her plump breast and declared, "Why, I don't believe for *one minute* someone with a name like Jimmy Doolittle has dropped a bomb on Tokyo, Japan!" While fields of Kentucky burley burst into pastel blooms, America fought the Battle of the Coral Sea and won the decisive battle of Midway, and before the end of that year, before Joe Collins could even strip out the crop and send it off to the Grower's Market, we would add Dieppe, El Alamein, Salerno, and Anzio to the list of strange-sounding names. While FDR made war on Admiral Yamamoto in the Pacific, Doc made war on FDR and sang Sir Winston Churchill's praises. He quoted the cocky PM with a big cigar, "Now there's a man for you!" Doc beamed. "Not your goddamned silky with his cape and a foot-long cigarette holder!"

Pastels

I DON'T MIND TELLING YOU, the war was of no concern to me that spring of 1942. I was almost seven and in the third grade and I had my own problems. Lunch box worries, for example.

In late springtime, the third-grade day students situated themselves within a well-pruned circle of boxwood to eat lunch beside a small pool of lotus lilies and Japanese goldfish. A delicate stone statue of Saint Francis of Assisi stood nearby, and every now and then a warm breath of air swept pale strands of weeping willow over the dark pool to gently brush his face and the bird in his outstretched hand. Seated beside the lily pool, little Miss Perfect Lucie Cross Dunlap and Trinette Bigsby, the teacher's pet, opened their pretty pastel lunch boxes and traded olives for slender celery or carrot sticks. Someone had taken time to carefully trim the crusts of their little Philadelphia Cream Cheese sandwiches and to wrap them neatly in Cut-Rite wax paper, and there was always a little bunch of seedless grapes. They bartered a brownie dusted with powdered sugar for a chocolate chip or oatmeal cookie but, believe me, nobody negotiated for the fare in my pail. At *my* house, Eva Belle Twyman saw that lunch pails were packed each morning and set out on the back porch for Joe and me and the six or eight hired men who worked on the farm.

Like those men who broke their backs working in the tobacco, time and hard wear left the clumsy old metal boxes scarred and bent. Some of the latches were missing, some were rusty, and I was humiliated to take one of the relics to school, much less open it up and reveal enough food to feed a hungry farmhand. The girls snickered at my slab of ham on a cold biscuit the size of my hand or at greasy fried chicken, and Lord knows, I never revealed the slice of leftover breakfast mush I occasionally discovered on the bottom of the rough old pail.

"Why can't I have a lunch box like everybody else? Maybe a green one with a thermos instead of this piece of scrap," I whined to Joe, nudging the old box with my dusty ankle-boot. "Lucie Cross has a yellow one with pansies painted on it and Trinette's is red, white, and blue with gold stars. *Everybody* has a pretty little lunch box, everybody!" I sniveled. He pondered the lunch box predicament for a bit. "Well, you're not just everbody, Pig, are you now." He looked off a little in his familiar way, "You know what Miss Eva Belle says, 'Beauty's only skin deep, ugly goes to the bone, beauty dies and fades away but, ugly, Pig, it holds its own.'" He recited the little poesy with great pride, then added: "We don't need the lunch pail talk and don't go judging a book by its cover." So *that* matter was closed.

The Pale Pink Tutu

THAT SPRING, RIGHT BEFORE the May Day gala—without a doubt, the biggest event at my school—Aunt Sudie Louisa told the Buck Pond Duplicate Bridge Club girls about the rug. "I suppose it's all over town by now that Cousin Dot Harriss gave the magnificent Chinese rug, of all things, to those nuns at the school! They've put it in the front hall, right under that big brass crucifix!" She could *not* get off that Chinese rug business. Not for one minute!

Doc said Sudie expected the rug would come to her along with the silver and china and the shares of Co-Cola stock when our oldest relative finally gave up the ghost at ninety-eight, but the lady left everything she had to our peculiar Cousin Dot and to the Episcopal School for Girls. Aunt Sudie Louisa fumed at the injustice, she railed at the lawyer who read the will, and then she took off on the innocent nuns of the Episcopal Order of Saint Anne. "I thought those nuns took a vow of something or other and it didn't include a Chinese rug that belongs right this minute in the museum in New York City, not to mention three sterling-silver service sets and fine French china." And she never failed to add, "Who in this world would have guessed she would leave the portraits, fine linens, and half the Co-Cola stock to Dot of all people, as if she could get one more cup and saucer in that cavernous house of hers. Why, leaving Dot one red cent is like carrying coals to Newcastle, I'm here to tell you. Everybody knows she has more money than God!"

Our odd cousin Dot Harriss was also known to have a germ fixation. She wasn't afraid of the devil himself or lightning storms or gypsies or the tramps that came to the back door to ask for food and scared the daylights out of Eva Belle and the Aunties. She feared only tiny germs she couldn't see. She claimed she never used a bar of soap twice, and she was so terrified of inhaling or swallowing a disease that she spit all the time. It was mean of Sudie to claim Dot was invited to attend the May Day carrying-on at my school just because she gave the Chinese rug to the nuns, but everybody knew Sudie had a mean streak a mile wide. "Well, that's Sudie for you," they said, and they just let her run on about whatever she had in her craw. But I always thought my pretty Aunt Sudie Louisa was mean because she was just plain scared of *everything*.

Cousin Dot arrived to attend the May Fete that unusually warm afternoon in late May dressed in an ankle-length mink, with white gloves halfway up to her elbows. She was spitting even as she was being escorted to her front-row seat. Doc and Joe had chauffeured her to my school, handed her off to the nuns, and retired to the rear of the assembly to light up their great big Cuban cigars. Sallie Gay and the Aunties had a spell—and I didn't blame them—when they saw Dot's outfit, not to mention the spitting, and she was seated on the front row for all the world to see.

Dressed in my pink tutu, satin slippers on my feet, and a bouquet of sweet peas in my hair, I was in Sallie Gay's pretty world for a moment. She stood smiling beside Aunt Tott and Sudie Louisa. "So *sweet* and *clean,*" they sighed as I glided down the front stairs, my head tilted to one side, my hand lightly brushing the polished handrail. Eva Belle shook her head and asked, "Well, I declare, who is this sweet little girl?" Joe put his hands on his hips and grinned, "Is that you, Pig? What you got on your head? Sweet peas?" Never was so much attention heaped so freely on a child for just bathing and putting on a little pale pink organdy and satin. *At last,* my stylish Sallie Gay and the Aunties thought, *the child is one of us.* Sweet-smelling and clean like the other third graders, like Lucie Cross, freckled, and done up in a yellow tutu with daisies in her auburn corkscrew curls. They beamed with pride and relief as I nimbly stepped into the hall, assumed the third position, my hands in a graceful curved arch above my bowed head. "Ah…Oh…" they whispered. I itched, I could not sit, and I could not disturb the sweet peas to scratch my head.

At last, I would be a butterfly and dance around the Maypole. My sheer organdy wings trembled in the breeze as I tiptoed through the boxwood garden and across the manicured lawn, to take my place at the foot of the flagpole braided in delicate colored ribbons blowing like rainbow streamers in the early summer afternoon.

I was the smallest. I stood in the middle of eleven more pastel butterflies fluttering and shimmering around me. We awaited our signal from Sister Mary Theresa: she tilted her head and opened her hands just like the statue of Saint Francis by the fishpond. With our cue to deep curtsey, twenty-four quivering gossamer wings and a fresh flower garden of peonies, pansies, and sweet peas, we bowed in unison and scurried on tiptoe to assemble for the Butterfly Dance. Finally, presentation was at hand, and I'm here to tell you, you could have heard a pin drop on the new mown grass.

Dear moon-faced Mrs. Alice Pelham Nottle, the former headmistress, came in late and was crammed in right next to Dot. Despite her attempts to perch as lightly as possible on the fragile wooden chair, it creaked and swayed beneath her weight and dug its flimsy legs into the soft carpet of grass. I was embarrassed at the thick cloud of Cuban cigar smoke curling above Joe and Doc in the back row, and I wished Sallie Gay, Tott, and Sudie would stop their waving and nodding and whispering and giggling. So here we come again, I thought. Unlike the other girls' families, who settled quietly, reverently into their places, we swooped in, as always, like a gaggle of geese to cause a commotion.

At last a hush settled over the gathering. Only the rustling of tutus in the warm breeze and a faint bird's song were heard when cousin Dot began coughing, sputtering, and spitting for fear of swallowing germs. In a desperate attempt to shift her bulk away from Dot's carrying on, Alice Pelham Nottle tumbled onto the grass. "Faugh, Oh, Faugh," she panted and cried, straining to right herself. Faculty and parents leaned forward in their chairs and craned their necks to see. Conversation broke out that someone was ill. "Is someone ill? Who could it be? Is the doctor here? Where is the doctor?" The nuns in pale gray habits ascended in unison from their seats and fluttered about like a flock of mourning doves over a baited wheat field. Aunt Tott, Sudie Louisa, and my mother threw up their well-manicured hands and cried out in unison: "Saints preserve us! Well, I never! Poor, Dot!" The unwitting Bishop, who was seated four seats away from Dot's spewing, bounded from his chair and raced to give aid. Kneeling at her side and taking her hand firmly in his, he thrust his handkerchief in her hand, and then turned to aid Alice Pelham Nottle, who still squirmed and struggled to right herself. Dot shot from her chair, flinging the Bishop's suspicious black handkerchief high in the air. The baby grand piano pealed strains of Chopin's *Waltz Brilliante,* and with her fur coattail flying, Doc and Joe whisked cousin Dot away to the sterile safety of her home. Our presentation was in chaos and the little butterflies stood motionless on the lawn. Everybody knew she was kin to me.

Part Two

Heaven's Little Footstool

THIRD GRADE BURST OUT of the starting gate at a dead run for summer. My mind raced with plans. I would drive the new John Deere tractor, sit around the artesian spring listening to Joe's tall tales after we worked in the tobacco, and once we were out of Sallie Gay's sight, I would climb on the running board of Doc's big silver automobile or smoke up a storm in the Grassy Springs truck or down in the tack room. I'd get my own Fink's overalls, ankle-boots, and four new red bandannas. Joe said, "Little Pig, you're going to be busier than a one-armed paperhanger!"

To me, summertime was a year long. That's the way of it when you are little, and I was little. I would be seven years old in August, and

I was by far and away the smallest of the third graders, who were all nine. When I was barely five, I stopped taking afternoon naps, my nanny Mattie H. left, and I was cast into first grade. I flushed my mother-of-pearl pacifier down the toilet. "Old passé is gone," I reportedly said. My mother watched in horror as gallons of water captured the precious heirloom and bore it away forever.

Joe Collins and I held a special reverence for the old crabapple tree which stood beside the flower gardens leading down to his cottage. In early summer, almost overnight, yellow-green buds burst into full bloom and I climbed to the very top to hide myself in her spray of pink and white. In June, iridescent lime-colored beetles the size of nickels arrived (Joe called them June bugs), and next came honey bees, butterflies, and hundreds of tiny blushing crabapples rushing to fill every inch of her dark branches until the old tree nodded beneath the weight. Later, those apples withered and dropped to the ground to draw swarms of black-and-yellow bees and brilliant emerald-green fruit flies. On summer evenings, Joe strolled down that old brick walk, past the flower beds of larkspur, baby's breath, and snapdragons that were strangely gray in the moonlight, and on toward the tree standing wide awake making her strange music. He stopped to light up a Lucky Strike and listen to the life sitting in her limbs. Peahens and peacocks clucked, guinea fowl screeched, while the buzz of tiny wings hovered just above the ground and covered the rotting apples like a busy cloud.

In June, Joe sent his crew into the hot humid fields to weed. "Take your grubbing hoes and weed good and close. You too, fat man," he told Daddy Rat Parrish, who claimed he was too stout to bend over and cut tobacco in the heat, much less climb the barn rails to house the stalks, and entirely too heavy to stand for hours in the stripping room making hands of tobacco. "You ease yourself in between those rows and try to put out a little work before you sit down to eat your dinner. And I *know* that's all you come for is Eva Belle's cooking," he added. On those hot summer days, men hoed out weeds from in between close rows of plants and Joe worried a hailstorm might rip the crop to shreds as the leaves grew broad and vulnerable and open to the sun.

I can see him now, standing in the middle of the patch dressed in his Fink's, hands on hips, bandanna tied around his neck, and the greasy Stetson set on the back of his head. If he could be here today, he would be the first to say there is no place on the face of this earth like our Heaven's Little Footstool: the gentle roll to the land; miles and miles of gray stone walls from another time meandering along shady lanes and pikes, beside rich fields where thoroughbred horses graze; Angus cattle with broad backs standing shoulder-deep in lush dark grass; black tobacco barns surrounded by acres and acres of green plants crowned by midsummer with shocking pink blossoms as large as Joe's round head. Joe Collins standing in the glorious pink: It's an image I will take to my grave.

Dale Evans

TIME AND AGAIN THAT SUMMER, my mother found me sitting under the shady porte cachere picking cinders and gravel from my bloody knees. "I don't know which one throws you down most, those mean ponies or your bicycle. They're all big enough for a grown man to ride." Aunt Sudie Louisa shared her opinion. "I have never ridden astride a *velo*." Sudie sprinkled French around to remind everybody she was a graduate of Miss Julia Tevis' Private Girls Academy, but it didn't impress me. Sallie Gay, Aunt Tott, and the entire Buck Pond Duplicate Bridge Club ladies had attended Miss Tevis' school. It's an antique gallery and lunchroom now. Doc said, "Sister Sudie Louisa lost all sight of herself after her *Grande Tour* of Europe when she was eighteen years old." My aunt spent an entire year over there and all she had to show for it was the banquet-size lace tablecloth from Belgium, some glass beads from Venice, and her teaspoon of French.

I can see Sallie Gay now, placing her small white-gloved hand on the handle of her blue Buick and turning to say, "Look at those knees, it's a wonder you have any knees left, isn't it?" Why did she ask questions that had no answers—questions like, "What am I to do with you? Do you want your mouth washed out with Ivory soap? What did I ever do to deserve this?" She stared at my ragged knees. "Please leave those rough neighbor-boys alone and go into the house so Eva Belle can tend to your knees. What's left of them," she added. "How did you hurt yourself this time?"

I ignored her question and asked, "Can I have a Flyer for my birthday, with a tote bar and a headlight and a horn with batteries?" She was dumbfounded. "Another wheel, I can tell you right now, is out of the question and what in the world is a toad bar?" "TOTE bar," I corrected her. "Whatever the thing is, the answer is no," she sighed. "Another wheel is out of the question. When your father gave you this one I said it was entirely too big for a little girl. A new one is the last thing in this world *you* need."

She was all worked up over the bicycle business. She turned her pretty head from side to side, and with renewed hope asked, "I'm going shopping with Tott and Sudie, don't you want *something* pretty from Tots and Teens?" She was seeing past my outfit, imagining me squeaky clean, done up in a scratchy dotted-swiss blouse with pretty ribbons in my hair. She hoped I would say, "I want a new dress, satin ribbons and white patents," but I couldn't get the words out of my mouth even though I knew how much they would please her. She wore a pale linen dress and her face was framed by a picture hat. I stood before her in a pair of faded shorts with two Ten-Cent Store pistols hanging down to my battered knees. I looked up from beneath the greasy brim of Doc's old Stetson hat, ragged guinea-hen feathers shooting out in every direction.

Joe Collins and I had rooted in the guinea-hen mess under the old crabapple tree until he found two gray- and white-speckled plumes almost a foot long that suited him. He wiped them clean with his bandanna and pushed them through the leather straps that ran the crown of my big hat. Nobody else in this wide world would have rummaged through those peahen droppings and flies with me. He used his penknife to slit holes in the wide brim, inserted a bootlace to tie under my chin. He set the hat on my head and stepped away from the old tree humming with June bugs and green flies to admire his work, spit a little tobacco juice onto the droppings, and bent down low so he could see up under the shady brim. "Does it bother you that you can't see out from under the hat?" he asked. "I guess not," he answered himself, "I know, sure as I'm standing here in this guinea-hen mess, that hat's not coming off you for love nor money." I wore the greasy Stetson that way for a month or more before he took time to pin up the front of the brim with a large safety pin. "Leastwise, this lets you see who you're talking to. That hat's *ready*, little Pig."

———

He always said "that's *ready*" when things just couldn't get much better. When he took his first sip of Eva Belle's fresh hot coffee in the early morning, he said, "Hot as hell, Pig, and black as night, that coffee is *ready*." At toddy time he tilted back his fine round head and let the bourbon slowly roll down his throat, "Good God amighty, little Pig, that twenty-year-old *medicine* can talk. That's *ready*." So I drank steaming hot, black coffee and I declared, "That's *ready*!" Fresh okra slid down my throat before I could get a good hold on it, or I ate pickled pig's feet with hot horseradish, and I swore "that's *ready*!" Eva Belle said, "If Joe Collins put two plump green tobacco worms on a cold biscuit, that girl would run do the same." Happiness for me was riding next to him, maybe twenty-five cents in the bib pocket of my overalls, a banged-up lunch pail between my feet, and the old hat in my lap.

She was disappointed with me. "How many pistols and big black holsters do you want? How many do you *have*?" She pointed a cautious finger. "And gloves big enough for a field hand. Why your father buys pistols, bicycles, and wild ponies that kick and bite I will never know." She glared at my gauntlets. They were heavily fringed, a sheriff's star blazed from the cuffs, and encircling the badges were gold letters: *DALE EVANS*. She was right, my gauntlets were three times too big for me. "He does it just to aggravate me, but there's no stopping him, oh no," she mumbled. "There's no stopping Doc."

A deep breath was all she required to press on. "Who would want a little girl all done up in these awful old clothes?" I knew the answer to *that* question alright, and it was Joe Collins and Eva

Belle Twyman. They didn't care what I wore or how dirty my hands and knees were. Eva Belle held both my hands and we touched our knees together under the kitchen table as she told tales of growing up on the farm with Doc. She placed a big ironstone crock of milk topped with inches of pure, rich cream on the counter, and I stood on a little stool beside her and carefully lowered the ladle. I learned to skim so lightly that only the sweet cream was caught up and the flecks of yellow left floating in the milk looked pale blue by comparison. We creamed chunks of churned butter with sugar and golden egg yolks and whipped our cakes in more old crocks. We baked cookies and breads, and she let me grind the beans and make Joe's coffee in the electric percolator, but no matter how many pots and pans boiled and sizzled in the kitchen, Eva Belle made time for me.

Sallie Gay was coming at it again. "The other girls in your class look so sweet in their pretty dresses. Do you think for a second they would run around with dirt ground into their knees and beneath their fingernails? Why don't you just plant potatoes under those nails and be done with it?" She came to a halt. "Oh, I can't get started on this." She brought a gloved hand to her bosom and sighed, "It makes me hot all over." But she regained her momentum. "Lucie Cross and Trinette do not play with those dirty, nasty boys." My eyes glazed over. I bet those two would give their eyeteeth to see the boys piss on a rock or a tree or a bug. And what would they give to play cowboys and Indians or tent out by the barn? Sweet little Lucie goody-two-shoes and teacher's pet Trinette set up a card table, put a blanket over it, and called it a tent. Hah! They crawled under it with a stuffed giraffe named Henry, a flashlight, and the bell from the dinner table so they could ring for help if the big bad bogeyman stuck his head in, and *that's* what they called camping out. Pitiful! But more than any of the games, I'll tell the world, they would like to play Doctor and Nurse and get themselves examined by the boys down in the cool, dark, secret cellar!

"There are plenty of girls who would give a share in the railroad to have the things you have never worn. You outgrew your white sandals without ever once putting them on your feet." She wasn't about to let it go. "Look at your feet, those awful boots. Maybe your nice things should be given to the unfortunate little girls at The Orphan's Home. How would you like that?" My heart leapt at the thought of unloading scratchy dotted swiss and Belgian lace. I longed to say, *Heave the little mink muff while you're at it,* but I said only, "Yes, Ma'am." At last, she stepped into the car, shut the heavy door, and placed her purse on the tufted seat. She turned to look at me and for an instant we stared deep into each other's eyes. The grinding of the engine cut through our moment and with a sigh she said, "Go brush your teeth and wash your hands...with soap."

She looked so defeated that I felt sorry for her—but not sorry enough to put on the scratchy dotted-swiss business and look pretty. "Pretty is as pretty does," Aunt Sudie Louisa was always saying and I wondered, What *does* pretty do? Sit like a doll in a china cabinet or under a card table with a stuffed toy and the dinner bell? Would it always be bloody knees or a greasy old hat that granted me her undivided attention? Riding ponies, bicycles, tractors, or shooting marbles in the dirt with the boys always brought on a sigh and an "I-give-up." How I wanted her to see me as more than a Dresden doll with a pretty painted face, and I prayed for a time when we would talk about more than clean fingernails and patent leathers. I dreamed of the days we would ride over the farm and I could tell her about our cattle and lambs, show her how to make hands of burley tobacco for market or how to hitch up the mules, one-eyed Kate and steady old Beck, and just maybe we wouldn't need to talk at all. I was there, beneath the greasy old hat with guinea hen feathers, tagging along behind Joe Collins, just waiting for her to really see me as Eva Belle and Joe saw me every single day. I could wait.

What Next, Child!

SALLIE GAY CONTINUED TO PLAY bridge and I continued to play with the boys. We knuckled down in the powdery dirt and shot marbles, firing away at each other, trading and lagging for the highly prized aggies, until one of us walked away with a full pouch, the earth ground deep into knees, knuckles, and nails.

Playing cowboys and Indians, I painted my body every color of the rainbow and rode hell-for-leather across the fields. I crouched in the weeds and in bushes, under shade trees, and in tall corn, panting, listening to my pounding heart. I waited, springing from my lair to attack the boys, bounding from the shadows, shrieking at the top of my lungs, riding bareback and sometimes backward, at a full trot after them, fearless, reckless, running wild.

One afternoon I overheard the boys planning to tie me to a tree and burn me alive. I climbed to my tree house and cut the rope ladder to ensure my safety. It never occurred to me to just pull up the ladder, or that I might be marooned in a rickety lean-to nailed to the bough of the old oak. As the sun dipped lower, I began to wonder how I would ever get down or make someone hear me. I was hungry and thirsty just thinking about supper, and the only rations in my roost were three cigarette butts, catalpa pods—which I smoked only in desperation—and a box of safety matches. For a change, I didn't feel one little bit like smoking. I would die of hunger and thirst, stuck up a tree on the very back of the property, out past my playhouse, well past Joe's green cottage, the smokehouse, henhouse, and beyond the barn. I called and called, but no one could hear my cries. Neither my mother nor Eva Belle ever came anywhere near these outbuildings. I imagined Eva Belle shelling peas and Sallie Gay somewhere with Tott bidding two hearts. The leap from the tree would break my neck. It would be *days* before they found me, crawling with maggots, like the dead birds I buried and then dug up each day to inspect for decay. The *Sun* weekly newspaper would tell the story on the front page: "Fall From Oak Tree in Back of Barn Kills Little Girl Just Shy of Seventh Birthday!" Foul play would not be overlooked; local police, Lexington police and detectives would question the strange little man called Squirrel Tooth who worked at the City Sewage Plant, tramps camping by the railroad trestle a mile away, and our tall, dark, silent mailman. Police would march down the aisle of the Lyric picture show and round up the *perverts* (anyone sitting alone), and question the boys from the pool hall. All my things would be given to The Orphans: my clothes, ponies, and the old mare I named Hot Flash for Aunt Sudie Louisa. At least that would comfort Sallie Gay, and maybe for the first time in her life Sudie Louisa would be sorry she never once in this world had the manners to thank me for naming the old pigeon-towed roan after her.

I would never celebrate my birthday on August 20th, I would never see fourth grade, I was done for. I went to sleep. I dreamed I heard the Grassy Springs truck pull into the barnyard but Joe never parked the pickup there. Maybe he was delivering hay or sweet feed for the ponies. It was almost dark. I hung out of the tree as far I could and screamed his name at the top of my lungs, "Joe, help me! Help me! It's Pig!" He didn't hear me. He was in the barn folding feed sacks, stacking them neatly in the corner, glancing around the tack room and the stalls to see if everything was in order for the night. I heard the feed-bin lids slam shut and the heavy metal latches thrown on the barn doors. He would light up a Lucky Strike, amble through the paddock and on up to his cottage, or to the house for supper, never knowing I lay stone-cold dead beneath the oak tree. Many years later he would shake his head and sigh to Eva Belle, "If only I had heard little Pig hollering at me from up in that tree..." But Joe stepped out of the barn and slowly walked in my direction, looking bewildered, cocking his head to one side. "It's me! It's me, *Pig*, stuck up in the tree!" I screeched his name until finally he saw the rope ladder piled on the grass and looked up to see me hanging out of the bough. He put his hands on his hips and shook his head slowly from side to side. "What *next*, Pig? *What next, child?*" It was an hour before they came and it seemed like forever, but two men from the fire department rescued me with long ladders just before darkness fell. Sallie Gay, Eva Belle, Joe, and his brother Dan gathered under the tree to watch the excitement. My life had been spared, but according to my mother I was headed for trouble with Doc for my reckless behavior. "You will tell him *everything* yourself. You will tell him exactly what you were up to this afternoon. *This time,* there is no telling what he will do!"

At the supper table, I told him every last detail, except the part about the butts, catalpa pods, and safety matches. Sallie Gay never touched one mouthful of food so intent was she, listening and nodding her pretty head in anticipation of Doc's iron hand. *"Killed,* she could have been *killed!"* she told him. "You must settle this child's hash or she is going to cripple herself *or worse."* Doc poured another glass of iced tea as he listened patiently to yet another account of my foolishness. "What else do those boys down at the firehouse have to do all day anyway?" he chuckled. "But why on God's green earth did you cut the rope?"

Joe Collins said, "Pig, you don't have to go *looking* for trouble, it knows just where to find you and it finds you every day." Aunt Sudie Louisa said I was "a brazen renegade child" when, shortly after the oak tree episode, I *borrowed* Joe's twelve-gauge shotgun, sneaked down the fencerow, and drew a bead on a tall purple ironweed plant in the middle of a pasture. I reached for the Winchester shells—also *on loan*—dropped one cartridge into the slick barrel, reached for number two, and slammed it home beside its ribbed twin. I snapped the gun shut and got a good grip on the stock, took careful aim, and pulled both triggers. I blew myself out into middle of the Pike, where the rural-route mailman found me unconscious. I wore my badly bruised face as a badge of honor, and when it faded to a greenish-yellow color, Joe laughed, "I swear, Pig, you've gone and turned the color of pond scum."

Sallie Gay told me, "You apologize to Joe Collins and you promise never to lay a hand on his possessions again," and quickly added, "say it like you mean it, too." She instructed Joe to keep his cottage "under lock and key." But Doc seemed more amused than concerned over my behavior. He winked behind his tortoise-shell glasses and told me I was the apple of his eye. Dear Aunt Tott fanned and agonized, "Do you think the little thing is a danger to herself?" Sudie Louisa pursed those pink lips of hers, wagged her tinted head, and warned, "Of course, she is a danger; she's a reckless little girl, and *she's just exactly like her father!*"

Muddy Bottom

I KNEW ANOTHER THING FOR SURE. I would be a farmer and tobacco grower like Joe Collins, delivering my calves and foals, baling hay for winter feed, and driving my truck over to the stockyards before dawn for breakfast at The Dew Drop Inn Cafe with the other cattle and Southdown sheep-breeders. One day I would drive the big Grassy Springs farm truck into town and the people standing in front of the courthouse or the ones going in and out of the C & D Market with their groceries would ask, "Is that the girl or Joe Collins?" Aunt Sudie Louisa continued to shake her tinted head and wag that pink manicured finger of hers in my face. "I declare, you act like you worship the very ground Joe

Collins walks on." Well, that was the Lord's truth then and it is true to this day.

I was already a lot like him. I ground dry golden tobacco leaves between my hands until I felt the heat, brought them to my nose and sucked in the bouquet, pressed my face against the mule's soft pink muzzle to smell dried bluegrass slobber around her old gray lips and on her breath while she wheezed in and out. I eased into the warm shadowy henhouse to eavesdrop on the muted clucking of Doc's prized white Leghorns, cupped a fresh egg in my hands, held it to my nose, and then rolled the warm egg down over my cheek. I buried my face in crates of butter-yellow baby chicks we ordered each spring. Velvety mule muzzles, Joe's piglets with stiff bristles for hair, and Grassy Springs broadleaf: I smelled them all and slipped away.

I ran through tall grass on still, summer days as startled grasshoppers with springs for legs exploded around me. Down by the clear, broad creek, bees hummed and dragonflies darted above the running water hurrying on its way to somewhere over smooth, mossy stones, under old willows and cottonwoods, past graceful black-green grasses that lay over the banks, swaying in the current. Deep pools were alive with skimmers, tadpoles, and crayfish. I discovered something busy and working hard beneath every rock or log. I let the cool, muddy bottom slip between my toes like feathers or fur, let myself sink into the mysterious ooze beneath me, as life throbbed in the willows and insects droned on the banks.

———

Where was the water rushing to, how did she survive violent summer storms that slashed and scarred deep into her banks, how did she suffer a long dry spell? Did this cool water run beneath our acres and acres of clover, bluegrass, and tobacco and then finally spill into the sweet, green Kentucky River? Did the creek spring from my granddaddy's ice-cold artesian well where Joe and I took our noonday meals? Did I?

The Pony Barn

I MUCKED OUT STALLS, hoisted bales of fresh straw and spread it deep and even as a carpet. My pony barn was small by barn standards—only three stalls, a tack room, a little tool room, and a loft upstairs—but it was my territory. I tiptoed up to the hayloft to spy on the ponies as they chewed oats and crunched ears of corn until a milky foam covered their black lips, and I listened to their halters clinking against the sides of heavy metal buckets as they sucked up half the water in the pail and flicked their ears at flies. I held *my* breath to hear *their* breathing. I wondered what they thought about. I studied Joe Collins as he ran his hands and the currycomb through long manes and tails, down their necks, and over their backsides, so I could do it just like he did. I eavesdropped on his gentle private talk as he lifted a pony's hoof, took a close look, and said, "By grab, you've gone and thrown another shoe alright."

My barn was a little world of breeding, hunting, and feeding. Feral cats dropped litters of hungry orange-and-white kittens to feed on soft gray mice that multiplied faster than you could count them, and the mice grew fat on oats and corn and the pony's sweet feed. Bats and barn swallows never wanted for spiders, bugs, or flies gorging on fresh pony dung. No wonder Sallie Gay never once set her slender foot in my barn. Under the eaves, I stretched out on my back and gazed up at cobwebs a yard wide, draped like flimsy lace in the corners or floating in the sunlight so I could see the nimble black-and-gold creature weaving her intricate trap. Slanted golden spikes of sunlight shot through knotholes and wide spaces between the boards above me and fell on the toe of my boot or lay in the palm of my hand, and then inched away from me, slipping over the straw to vanish. I breathed in time with the horses beneath me, while the fragrance of steaming manure floated up over me and out the open window. I was more straw and dust and sun than child in that place. I did not want to separate myself from the wildness of it and I grieved for my time there long before it was gone.

Now You Know

THE KITCHEN WAS A COMFORTABLE, worry-free room, its walls the color of rich custard. A slow paddle fan hung from the high ceiling. An old pine press at one end of the room held heavy crocks and ironstone platters, and a massive table topped with a three-inch slab of marble stood in the center. Eva Belle and I made fudge, sugar cookies, and gingerbread men on that table. She mounted the beaten-biscuit roller at one end and I could crank that elastic dough through the ringer until it snapped and popped. Afternoon sun poured in, supper simmered on the stove and baked in the oven, and her specialty, cloverleaf yeast rolls, rose from the heat of cooking and late sun.

Eva Belle Twyman was an elegant woman, graceful, tall, and slender, and like her mother, Miss Lula, she too was known as the finest cook in the county. She dressed in starched pearl-gray dresses and a white apron, with her hair caught up at the back of her head in a bun. Every week, she sang in the choir of the African Methodist church, often solos. The church Sewing Circle met in her home, and on Thursday nights she played five-card stud poker *with a vengeance.* She even did a little catering in her spare time. She never married and it's possible she was too strong for most of her suitors. "She's as independent as a hog on ice," Doc said. "If truth be told," said Joe, "Eva Belle's a little stuck on herself but that's alright too. Maybe she doesn't want anybody getting in her way or making a mess in her fine house."

Eva Belle brought her cup of coffee with a touch of cream to the table, wiped her hands with a tea towel, and arranged her apron carefully on her lap, patting it gently as she had laid it out just so. "All right now," she said under her breath and settled back in the chair. The sunlight over her shoulder gave off a warm radiance that encircled her head and her long smooth neck while she studied the light brown liquid in her coffee cup, as if answers might come floating to the surface to swim with the heavy cream. That same look was there when she worried and stewed over things, and it was there now, coupled with a dark shadow she couldn't tease away. She took both my hands in hers. "Well now, I've already told you I've known your daddy, Doctor Big Shot, since we were both little things." She lowered her head, furrowed her brow, and began working her mouth, rolling her lips in and out and moistening them from time to time. She drew a deep breath, closed her eyes, and slowly turned her head from side to side. She was trying to decide just where to begin her story.

"When your daddy was your age; now, let me see, I forget, how old *are* you now?" she teased. "Please don't tease, Eva Belle, tell about the terrible fall." I had long ago memorized the story but I held my breath every time she told it. "Well, he fell off backward from the high mantel in the front room and hit his head, hit good and hard, too, right on the stone hearth." Her eyebrows shot almost up to her hairline and she puckered up her mouth as if to say, "Now you know." The image of that boy flashed before me. I saw him high atop the mantel and then crashing onto the stones below. I held tighter to her hands as she spoke in a whisper. "He commenced to bleed like a stuck pig, his head split like you crack open a fresh egg from the henhouse. Everybody rushed to get the rig up to the house so that child could get to town and have himself sewed up."

I saw it all—the frantic household rushing to bring towels to my grandmother Anna to stop the awful flow of blood. I saw them running with the unconscious boy out the front door screaming, "Hitch up the rig!" I hardly took one breath while she spoke. "Well, they fixed his head and it healed itself up." I went limp with relief and slumped in my chair. "But!" She held up her long forefinger, again the brows shot up, and I felt the tightening return to my throat. "He ran around with both his eyes crossed-up for the better part of a year." A devilish grin slipped up on her. "We all laughed at him," she confessed, "and we sang, 'All join hands and circle round four eyes.'" I sputtered and giggled and was relieved of my tension for the moment. "He looked real simple with his light hair slicked down and parted right down the middle and those light eyes looking every which way, but thank the Lord, they straightened themselves out in their own time."

The dark look returned to her eyes. "When we poked fun, that brought on his temper spells. He cursed and kicked and jumped up and down like a little pea on a red-hot griddle, throwing himself around until his little legs gave out from under him and he would fall to the ground." She was whispering now and looking away from me, out to the lawn, as if she expected to see a small boy lying on the grass. Her eyes were sad when she looked back into mine. "That child just lay there, real still, till somebody came to carry him up to the house. We never knew if he wore himself out fussing or if it was that hit on the head."

She sat back and drew herself up straight. She slipped her hands from mine and stood beside my chair to tie a dangling ribbon at the end of my braid. She laid her hand gently on my head and then moved across the kitchen to the stove. "I'll tell the world, they threw away the mold when they made your daddy, Doctor Big Shot, and I've always said your granddaddy killed himself throwing a temper fit, just as sure as he put a gun to his own head, then pulled the trigger." She sat back down and this time she took my hands and turned the palms up to study the lines. Oh my, what did she see? My heart was going hard again. Some said Eva Belle had the sight. Will Middleton, the paperhanger from Pinkertown swore Eva Belle had a sixth sense, and Will should know: he could make a card table walk and he had a milky blind eye.

Did she see I would grow to be like my hell-raising granddaddy, running his fine horses into the ground, cursing the weather, and kicking the barn like my mean pony? Would I take after RM and be cursed with tantrums, likely to strike from out of the blue over a plate of kale greens? Did I inherit the burden of that temper as sure as my daddy had inherited his own fits along with the land? Would I go out in a fiery blaze? Or would I come to the end of my tether like Aunt Sudie Louisa, who many years later started singing along with the oscillating electric fan that played Episcopal hymns?

Eva Belle looked up at me and smiled. I finally drew a breath. "I can hear your mind racing and the worrying going on inside your head over what's to become of you, and I'm here to tell you, baby, if you don't stop tormenting yourself you sure to be old before your time." Thank the Lord she was smiling. "Now that's a real good sign, that line is," she murmured as she brushed her long fingers over the crease in my hand. "A long life and a happy one for this child," she declared. Her knowing eyes probed so deep it terrified me and I began to chew on the inside of my jaw. "Quit that screwing up your face!" she chided. "Won't you be a pretty thing if you were to go and freeze that way."

When I exhausted Eva Belle's patience with storytelling, I hounded Joe Collins to tell me about my granddaddy as we rode down the Pike in the Grassy Springs truck, or as we picked bushels of tomatoes for Eva Belle to put up in pale blue Mason jars. On rainy days I listened while we sat together on the old

Mammy's bench, cleaning saddles in the tack room. "Little Pig, I've told you about your granddaddy so many times I've set it to memory," he sighed. From time to time his recitals did sound singsong and I knew the tales were memorized, but I thrilled to those stormy days and the times I never knew. Eva Belle shot out her lip and said, "Joe Collins wouldn't know the truth if it was to meet him in the middle of the street," but he just laughed and told her, "I'm just sometimes careless with the truth, isn't that right, little Pig?"

They both agreed that granddaddy's temper took him right straight to the grave. In his younger days, he flew off half-cocked from the Bluegrass to Kansas in a Conestoga wagon. "That man took a fit one morning in Chastine's Barber Shop and by afternoon he set out for Kansas, of all things, swearing he would never return." They said he set out to follow the sun, leaving behind my grandmother Anna, and their two children, Aunt Sudie Louisa at ten and my daddy eight years old, to run the house and oversee seven hundred acres of farmland. Joe always told me, "You be proud they gave you your grandmother's name, Anna. She was the strong one; she ran that place and put up with him at the same time."

After driving a team of mules to the barren dusty flatlands of Kansas, RM took a good, hard, sober look and found himself ready to hightail it back home to the farm in the hot as hell summer of 1893. Somewhere out there, he unloaded the four-poster bed from the wagon, crawled under it with his little penknife with the pearl handle, and carved this inscription in the wood:

Sweet Jesus, take me safely home and I swear I will never leave
Kentucky again. So help me God. Signed, RMHH 1893.

I was never really sure if RM did his carving beneath the stars in a far away place called Kansas, but every night I slept under a soft white canopy in that big bed, and behind the ruffled bed skirts his prayer was etched deep in the wild-cherry wood.

Joe laughed and said, "That old man, he was still stuck on himself at eighty-six years. Your Aunt Sudie comes by that business fair and square." To the end, they said, his dapper appearance was his pride and joy, and he didn't care one bit who knew it. He was imposing, with a thick shock of wavy white hair down to the shoulder. He called it his crowning glory. In the summertime, he strutted around the town in his linen suits and fine Italian neckties, refusing to place a hat on his glorious head, but he carried a soft, sweet-smelling Panama along with his walking stick, just for show. He sashayed about in winter dressed in a greatcoat that hung to his ankles, with its wide collar trimmed with Persian lamb. Everybody knew he was nothing more than a cantankerous old farmer, but he raised so much commotion they gave him a wide berth.

He never let on that he suffered from high blood. "Most likely brought on by his bad disposition," according to Eva Belle. "They said it hurt the old man's pride to admit he had a nasty little cancer on his lower lip, and both knees full of birdshot." The high blood gave him a deep blush that made a dramatic background for his untamed, white eyebrows and the wild mustache that rested above his upper lip, like a white dove ready to take flight. Whenever the notion took him, he whipped out his little tin of English wax and commenced twisting and dabbing at it, twist and dab, twist and dab, until the ends shot out straight as arrows. "It's the Lord's truth," Joe said. "He could not keep his own hands off it for love nor money." RM was driven into town each morning, right up to the front door of Chastine's Barber · Shop in the New Woodford Hotel. He sat himself down in chair number one, next to the window looking directly across to the courthouse, while little Chastine himself pruned, snipped, and waxed the noble brush.

They claimed he woke up mornings just itching for a good fight, thundering like Moses, laying down his own commandments. In the end, he went out like thunder and a bolt of lightning in the scorching heat. It came as no surprise that he was taken in the midst of one of his tantrums. The fatal one came on him during lunchtime. Joe said, "He lost himself over a plate of Miss Lula's kale greens of all things. To the end, kale was his favorite dish."

Miss Lula, Eva Belle's mother, was RM's friend since childhood, and they grew up together on Grassy Springs Farm. That hot summer day, Old Man blew through the swinging kitchen door and into her kitchen, a plate of kale clinched in his hand, swearing at the top of his lungs: "It's hot enough to fry a gaddam egg on the sidewalk in town on the Main Street!" He stopped just long enough to take a breath as he slammed down the plate. "I might nigh choked to death on your red peppers, on your dose from hell!" He thrust his glaring face into Miss Lula's face and squinted his pale blue eyes: "That's what I call your cooking, a gaddam dose from hell." He yanked at his silk necktie, purple veins in his neck bulging, and he was soaked right down to his skin, into his collar, down his back. "Couldn't get his own breath an' still he ran on at Miss Lula over kale greens," Joe sighed.

Miss Lula met him head on, wagging a kitchen spoon in his furious, florid face. She was not intimidated by him or by the devil himself. "Ole Man Temper's got you good this time, *huh? Huh? HUH?*" she scolded. "And you are fixing to have yourself a fine one, I can see that alright." She stepped closer until they were almost toe-to-toe. "I say, Old Man Temper will take you one fine day sure as I am standing here." Her outburst added more fuel to his fire. He twisted a smirk on his face and reached for the ultimate insult to the woman he had known since childhood, to the finest cook in the county. "I wouldn't feed this kale to a hog and God knows, I cannot tolerate a hog!" Miss Lula snatched up the heavy cast-iron pot containing the remains of the kale greens and flew at him. "You ugly-acting old man, you take yourself right out of my kitchen this minute or else!" She sloshed the pot at him while she backed him through the screen door, out onto the porch, and down the back steps. He scurried away from her and was standing knee-deep in the cucumber patch before she let go her hold on the pot, spilling its greasy contents onto the bed of red and orange zinnias bordering the garden. The two of them slumped like a pair of old dogs, glaring at each other across the little hills of cucumbers and flaming flowers. His breathing came harder and he was wringing-wet from doing battle in the blistering heat, but determined, as always, to have the last say. "This time you've done it, by God," he gasped, "gone an' got yourself fired good and proper this time!"

He snatched the little penknife with a pearl handle from his vest pocket, yanked up a cucumber, partially peeled it, and took a bite. "Be one cold day in hell before I'll eat your cooking again," he fumed, jabbing at her with the little knife, and then true to his word, my granddaddy pitched over stone-cold dead in the patch, his penknife in one hand and a pickling cucumber in the other.

If That Don't Beat All

MISS LULA SAID SHE WOULD take the awful sight of him stretched out in the cucumbers and zinnias to her own grave. The trauma gave her a bad case of the hives but she put on a fine wake for RM, directing additional cooks and waiters, seeing that white linen tablecloths and napkins were washed and ironed to perfection by Miss Ermine Grundy. Ermine Grundy had always frightened RM by telling him she was half-Cherokee, and he admitted he was half scared of her peculiar ways. As fortune would have it, he was laid out in the study, usually cool and restful in the hot summertime, but located directly over Ermine Grundy's laundry room.

———

They laid him out in his best suit and set the big bronze coffin in the middle of the room, "right on the fine Per-shun rug," Joe said. His glorious head of shoulder-length white hair and the theatrical mustache had been groomed and waxed for the last time by Chastine. RM never looked better. Comfortable old leather chairs faced the fireplace, and the walls held pictures of horses and faded photographs. Bookcases were filled with binders that held farm accounts, records of cattle breeding and tobacco sales; there were leather-bound volumes of William Shakespeare, often misquoted by RM, and histories of The Commonwealth of Kentucky. A large black-and-white photo of RM and the farm's prize bull, Big Business, hung directly over his mahogany desk. A paddle fan hung suspended from the high ceiling. Chairs and tables with starched white cloths were set on the freshly pruned lawn beneath the shade trees. Flowers of every description filled the house. Waiters wore jackets starched so heavily by Ermine Grundy they could hardly bend their arms to serve the drinks, and they swished from room to room offering trays of food. Doc broke out RM's fine cigars. Cooks baked hams, hot rolls, and cakes. The sideboard groaned with aspics, fried chicken, and guinea hens. RM would have loved it: he was known as a big spender.

The more the crowd enjoyed the deceased's liquor in the sweltering heat, the more they remembered him as a force to be reckoned with, and exaggerated tales of his carrying on buzzed throughout the house and out onto the lawn. The Mayor's wife burst into uninvited song and her discordant strains throbbed from the once-peaceful study to invade conversations outside. It was a magnificent production, and come to find out—RM planned every detail. He selected the bronze casket, chose his best white linen suit and Italian necktie, and left extensive directions for the elaborate wake. He instructed his barber to trim his crowning glory and wax the dramatic mustache for the last time. He was to lie in state receiving visitors for three days. He charged them not to embalm him under any circumstances!

The temperature hit ninety-five and was on the rise by afternoon of the very first day. Coupled with the unbearable humidity, it was likely the old man would not keep. Doc met with the Rexall druggist and the undertaker in secret out on the back porch to discuss the critical situation; the druggist would prepare gallons of topical embalming elixir immediately. Late at night, after the last caller had signed the leather-bound book in the front hall, the mortician, Doc, the druggist, and Joe Collins were to apply it to the remains. "Thank the Lord, that old man held. Lord *love* him," Joe told me, shaking his head in disbelief, remembering it as if it had happened only yesterday.

Throughout the wake, the Indian woman's chanting and moaning seeped up to RM laid out on the Persian rug. Joe said, "The Indian woman took bones, chicken heads and feet, wrapped them up in a little bag of cheesecloth, and hung that dirty mess over the laundry room door." Ermine Grundy declared, "Old man death is on the prowl in this house and he is not about to come through my laundry room door."

The Indian Woman was the most mysterious human being a girl could ever hope to know. While Miss Ermine chanted and swayed over the ironing board, I would fill the six-foot tub in the laundry room to almost overflowing, take a good deep breath, and throw myself face-down to practice the Dead Man's Float, until Ermine finally grabbed me by the back of my bathing suit and hauled me out to dry. "Stop that trying to drown yourself or I'll run you through the washing machine wringer till you're dried out good and proper!" I would continue my floating and she'd mumble over my submerged head, "That's not natural, the child's not right. Most curious child. *Oomph, oomph, oomph.*"

Deep creases in her dark face pulled the corners of her mouth down toward a sharp chin bristling with long black curly hairs; glass beads, chicken feathers, and yellowed squirrel's teeth dangled around her wrinkled neck, and strange articles swung from her long, tissue-thin ear lobes. Her hair was braided and hung in a queue down to the small of her back. But the Indian woman's most extraordinary feature was what Joe Collins called "The restless eye." The left one held you in a steady gaze while its partner scanned walls and ceiling, poking itself into the corners of the laundry room. Joe said, "Don't let the eye light on you, Pig. Miss Ermine wouldn't set out to do harm, but that restless eye, well, it wants to go on its own."

By the end of the second day, RM's wake turned itself into a three-ring circus. Despite his directives, they cut it short, and not one moment too soon. On the morning of the third day, they disturbed him for the last time, drove him down the McCracken Pike, and laid him out in the quiet coolness of Glen's Creek

Christian Church, where he was baptized as a boy. The ill-informed preacher eulogized RM as:

> *A generous man, a good neighbor, and a loyal friend, who enjoyed companionship but shrank from crowds. A kind and indulgent father, a man of strong affections. And those who knew him best were those who loved him most: a quiet peaceful man whose gentle ways would be sorely missed. Our brother, Richard Moses Harriss Holt, slipped this mortal coil peacefully in his sleep.*

Miss Lula sighed out loud, "NOW IF THAT DON'T BEAT ALL!"

Gas

MISS LULA WAS BORN on the Grassy Springs Farm on the Grassy Springs Pike, just six months after my granddaddy. Grassy Springs Pike was a shady lane then with fields of grasses on either side—grasses so thick in the lush Kentucky summer they waved like a black-green sea. Thick hedgerows of brambles outlined pastures where cattle and horses and his Southdown sheep grazed. The farm was separated from the Pike by a stone wall, three feet high, and simple stone columns flanked the entrance to an avenue lined with oaks leading back to the brick house.

Half a lifetime later, Miss Lula and RM would survive the worst wind and hailstorm to ever strike the Bluegrass. The storm moved in at sunset. Not a leaf stirred in trees lining the drive before the wind roared onto the place with full force, raining hailstones the size of walnuts. According to RM's farm journal: "Cattle, horses, and sheep in the fields went to their knees trying to get a hold on the earth. My barns that survive stand without double doors, front and rear."

I imagined his great tobacco barns standing naked, with their mouths open wide, as if they had sucked in their breath when the wall of wind came at them. With daybreak, I saw breezes trailing in and out of the barn vents, spiraling around the old Poplar beams, saw my granddaddy standing on his front porch squinting in the early light, and thundering, "Good God almighty." Not one tree was left standing.

RM was a young man in his forties then, his light hair tied at the nape of his neck, dressed in tall boots and a whipcord jacket for bird-shooting. A leather riding whip dangled from his right hand and he unconsciously slapped it against his boot. Stepping from the porch and down the brick steps, he moved like a man on his way to a hanging. That storm snapped tree roots and left two-hundred-year-old oaks and beeches lying face-down in mire; it stripped his barns and shredded each broad leaf of tobacco. But he rebuilt every last inch. He repaired the barns and put up new ones with larger stripping rooms, planted fifty additional acres of tobacco, and then turned around and dug a three-acre lake. And out behind the stable, well beyond the house, RM built himself a trotting track. After toddy time, in the early evenings, they say he whipped around that dusty oval, driving like a wild man, hollering and laughing until horse and driver dragged to a steaming halt, both of them in a lather.

"After your grandmother Anna passed," Joe said, "those two old friends went at it hammer and tong. Miss Lula quit him for a pastime." She declared the kitchen was her domain, hers and hers alone, and she informed him she would not tolerate his bad disposition. When he did misbehave, she slammed her cast-iron skillets over the sharp edge of the marble table and told him, "I quit, and this time for good!" Within a week or ten days she always cooled down, but only after RM sent peace offerings around to her house.

He sent a box of Roi Tan cigars or a sack of red-hot sage sausage—that was her favorite, and she knew he usually saved it for himself. Once he sent her a milk cow and had it tethered in her backyard out by the privy, and after a week passed and not a single word was heard from her, he went out to the house. To his surprise, the milk cow was gone. "I sold it," she told him, "bought myself a washing machine with a wringer." And there it sat, in her parlor, with a pretty pitcher of fresh flowers on it. "What would I want with that cow?" she scolded. "You ought to know by now, I don't take milk, it gives me gas." She didn't take any lip off my granddaddy or anybody, and she took her good sweet time but she did come back to knead her buttermilk biscuits and to smack the cast-iron skillets on the thick marble slab.

Tight as Dick's Hatband

WHEN THE CENTER HELD, we had good times, but we just never knew when things might come to a boil, when Doc would loose himself again and our life would explode like lead shot from the barrel of a twelve-gauge shotgun. I was thankful when the moon-faced clock that hung above the pine press in the kitchen said six-thirty in the morning and Eva Belle tied on her apron, and I dreaded that time in the evening, about eight-thirty or nine o'clock, when she told Joe, "You can carry me on home now." So I did anything I could think of just so they might stay one minute longer.

———

One hot summer evening, as Eva Belle fussed over the last of the pots and pans, I sat at the kitchen table with Joe, while he sipped his last cup of coffee and smoked a Lucky Strike. He took a good hard look at me. "Those front teeth of yours are getting too big for their own good. I swear, I don't believe I've ever seen teeth like that on a child your size." He was halfway kidding me but it was true. The big front teeth shot out over my lower lip, and when I tried to shut my mouth, Joe told me, "Pig, you look like you got yourself a mouth full of pennies." That did it. Without a *by your leave,* I marched right across the room, straight as an arrow, to the box of large safety matches on the counter, removed four of the sticks, rammed all of them between the big front teeth, and lit myself up.

"She's at it again!" Eva Belle screamed when she saw my mouth ablaze. "Help me to put the child's mouth out." Joe jumped up from his chair, spilling his coffee and sending the cup sailing over the floor and clear into the pantry. He yanked up a tea towel and came at me to smother the flames, swearing, "Good God amighty, what's she trying to do, lighting up her head like that!" Eva Belle grabbed another towel and started fanning, "Could've set her whole self on fire." "Don't talk," Joe declared, shaking his head in disbelief, "don't talk to me about this child."

They stared at me, still shaking their heads. "What got into you *this* time?" Joe asked. "Foolish, foolish child," Eva Belle murmured. "I worry she won't make it through the summer." Meanwhile the acrid fumes floated up my nose and down my throat, my eyes watered, and I began to cough and cry. In his frenzied attempt to extinguish my flames, Joe's big fist and the tea towel jammed the partially burnt matchsticks securely into my bucked teeth and they were stuck fast.

Eva Belle sat down next to me at the table and soothed, "Now, now baby, what's done is done, and looks like you didn't even get yourself singed." She directed her full attention to my mouth, cautiously grasping the front match and attempting to wriggle it loose. "They're stuck in there tight as Dick's hatband," she said, looking up at Joe.

"Let me at those ivories," he told her. "If I can't work a kitchen match loose from Pig's front teeth, then my name's not Joe Collins." He knelt down beside me, wiped his hands on his overalls, and got a good purchase on the stick. "Hold yourself still." One by one he worked them loose and I felt the big teeth relax. He stood up, dropped the burned, broken matches on the table, and then he looked close again. "Looks to me like you got *more* room between the big front ones now. Little Pig, you won't do." Eva Belle sighed as she put on her hat. The moon-faced clock on the kitchen wall said almost ten o'clock.

Something's Fishy

TIME MEANT LITTLE TO DOC when it came to answering a patient's call for help. He left the house any time of night or day. One night in July, the Chief of Police telephoned. The town's new Chief was a friendly young man named Jim Ed but everybody called him Scooter. He preferred Chief. He was chubby, pink-faced, and crammed into his slick, new, dark blue uniform like the piggy sausages Zack and Daddy Rat packed in tight casings at hog-killing time. His blue shirt was too little and his pants were too long. Joe Collins said, "Scooter's new uniform britches fit him like socks on a rooster."

―――――

Chief Jim Ed—Scooter—took his job too seriously, and on that night in July, while he was patrolling down around South Main Street, he discovered a suspicious light burning in the back room of the United States Federal Post Office. The young lawman scurried back to the courthouse a block away to make his telephone calls for help. "This is Central. What do you want, Scooter?"

Central was the Bell Telephone Company operator, Elsie Mae, who was housed in a small room over the Railway Express Office on Main. To place a call I picked up the heavy black receiver and tapped the button. "It's Elsie Mae, honey, you want to call your daddy's office?" Doc's office was 2, and as soon as Elsie heard Miss Lucy Hunter say, "Doctor's office, Lucy Hunnah," she jumped right in there, "Here's your daddy's office, honey, and how're you, Lucy?"

Elsie Mae was a very important person in the town since every single solitary call went through her, and of course, she was privy to every conversation. Aunt Sudie Louisa liked to say, "Elsie Mae is a nosey know-it-all." Sallie Gay agreed that Elsie Mae probably did know it all. "You can't blame her for eavesdropping, just sitting there as she does, all the livelong day and sometimes at night, connecting numbers, for goodness sakes."

"Elsie," Scooter said, "get me Doc. I want to tell him there's something, well, *fishy* down at the Post Office." He lowered his voice to a whisper, speaking out of the corner of his mouth. "We might need him if there's, well, trouble." He dropped his voice another octave: "There's a light on in the back room." *"A light's on!*" Elsie shrieked through the receiver. "*Somebody's in there I'll bet . . .* Here's Doc, hello Doc, it's Elsie Mae. There's . . ." Scooter drew an exasperated breath. "Forevermore, Elsie, *I'm* paid to do this job and I'll tell him what's the matter my own self. Doc, it's Chief down at the courthouse and there's a very suspicious light on in the Federal Post Office . . . in the back room. I believe you should come on in case there's trouble." Hoping Elsie wouldn't hear, he whispered, "You know what I mean." "Scooter, you better run get yourself a couple of boys from the pool hall right this minute," Elsie blared again. "I'll be right on," I heard Doc say. "And, Scooter, I think you should tell Elsie Mae to get Judge Lamont on the telephone while you're at it." "Over and out," Scooter replied and flashed for Elsie. "I'm already ringing the Judge," she assured him. "I figured as much," he sighed.

"Light's on in the Post Office," Doc told Sallie Gay. "Miss Edwina might have left her lamp on, but if she did it will be the first time in thirty years she overlooked something." (Miss Edwina ran our United States Federal Post Office on Main Street with an iron hand; she stepped right in and took over her husband's position the very week poor Harry Bright went to an early grave at forty-one. Fulfilling her duties as Postmistress was her life.) "Little Scooter says there might be trouble. I doubt that, but I'll go on in. Almost too hot to sleep anyhow," he added. I was beside him. "It's almost too hot to sleep," I echoed, and begged him to let me go with him. "Why not?" he answered, and my astonished mother fumed, "I cannot believe for one minute that you are taking that child into town in the middle of the night."

———

As we slipped into our robes, she was still insisting I belonged in bed, and she was still carrying on as we padded down the front stairs in soft slippers. "What if that little policeman, that Scooter or whatever they call him, is right for once, what if there *are* bandits in the Post Office. Mercy!" Her admonitions echoed as we went into the summer night, just the two of us, riding into town for an adventure in our pajamas.

The silver La Salle eased into a parking space directly across from the United States Federal Post Office as Judge Francois Emile Lamont's big black car purred up behind us. He was dressed in his nightclothes, too. He moseyed over in velvet house slippers with the letter *L* sewn in gold. He placed his gold-monogrammed foot on the running board of the La Salle. "What do you want to bet Miss Edwina left her lamp on?" "That's what I think, Meale," Doc agreed. (The judge's name was Emile—he was French way back—but Doc called him Meale to his face, and Little Dandy or Silky behind his back.) I hurled myself into the back seat to get a better look as the three men approached the foreboding Federal Post Office.

The uniformed policeman and two volunteers from Floyd's Pool Hall cautiously climbed the steps, and my imagination took over. I saw the massive bronze doors at the top of those stairs fly open and gunmen dressed in long black overcoats and fedoras bolt from inside the United States Federal building with machine guns, shooting everything in sight. I saw the bloody Chief tumbling down those wide steps, his gun still clutched in his hand. My heart raced. I watched as the boys from the dirty pool hall were riddled with bullets. The band of gangsters rushed past the fallen men, across the street, up to our car, and circled us, pointing their machine guns at Doc. "Drive us to McKee's Crossroads or to Nonesuch or Pisgah or out to Troy or else!" The *Sun* headlines read: "Doctor and His Little Girl Kidnapped by United States Federal Post Office Bandits." But Scooter and the boys ambled up the steps and the little Chief opened the bronze door with a key. They walked inside to find Miss Edwina's forty-watt lamp on. "Looks like Miss Edwina left her lamp on," Scooter yelled across to us, "but thanks for coming in, Doc." "That's alright. It's almost too hot to sleep anyhow," Doc told him. "What did I tell you," Judge Meale said. "A lot of silly carrying on in the middle of the night."

Doc turned over the engine and asked right out of the blue, "How about an Orange Crush up at The Sweet Shop?" He wheeled the big car around in the middle of the street as I reached over him and tooted the horn to Judge "Silky" Meale. We waved goodbye to Scooter and the boys, headed straight up Main Street to The Sweet Shop across from the courthouse, and parked right in front since we were the only car on Main in the middle of the night. Lucky for us, Big Tootsie Sizemore was staying late to polish the chrome on his soda fountain, refill the ice-cream containers, and unload two cases of Dr Pepper and Orange Crush. We marched straight to the gleaming soda fountain and climbed up on the slick red-leather stools trimmed in chrome. I told Big Tootsie *everything* about the light Miss Edwina left on and the thugs who might have shot up the Federal Post Office as he poured Orange Crush in tall glasses with crushed ice and gave us two red-and-white-striped straws apiece. "You're stealing little Scooter's thunder," Doc said. "Scooter will be talking about the light business till Christmas... of next year." He handed Tootsie a nickel. "Play that one Dorothy Shay sings, I forget what you call it." "'Feudin' and Fightin',''' Tootsie told him. "It's on the Top Ten in the Hit Parade, Doc. You picked yourself a winner." Tootsie was beaming from ear to ear as if Doc had just won a six-furlong longshot race over at the Keeneland race track. "Whatever," Doc mumbled as the gleaming silver-and-glass jukebox came alive, flashing every color of the rainbow over the walls and across the face of the soda fountain mirror as Dorothy Shay belted out "Feudin' and fussin' and a-fightin', this is a wrong that needs a rightin'."

The clock above Tootsie's curly carrot-topped head said ten minutes till ten, but to me it was the middle of the night. I was *never* up past dark. What had got into my daddy? It was all too wonderful and Tootsie said he would not take one single red cent for the orange drinks. We shook his hand and Doc told him, "You're a good man, Big Tootsie, you do a good job." The pat on the back pleased Tootsie. "You just keep coming in for a soda, Doc, and playing Dorothy Shay on the jukebox, too." "Whatever," Doc mumbled again, and we slipped down from the red stools and went once more into the night as Doc muttered, "Nobody ever claimed Big Tootsie was heavy-headed."

I rode all the way home from The Sweet Shop on the running board of the silver La Salle, my pigtails and summer pajamas blowing in the breeze, just the two of us, prowling those dreamy lanes, in our pajamas, in the middle of the warm summer night.

The Playtex Panty Girdle

THAT AUGUST OF 1942 broke all records: temperatures shot past 100 and stayed there, electric fans hummed day and night, the Rexall Drug Store couldn't keep the ice cream and sherbet frozen, and my Aunt Tott was widowed at forty-four. Joe said, "Your Uncle Freddy stepped out to the porch after supper, sat down with the newspaper, and went out like Lottie's eye! The sight of it laid your Aunt Tott out flat as a flitter on the porch floor, right next to her Freddy, still sitting upright in his chair."

Aunt Tott and Pearl were all alone now in Tott's big house. The two women had been together since Pearl had learned to cook and Tott to plan a menu, over twenty years. "I'll tell the world," Pearl said, "we've seen it all and we've seen it through together." They stood side by side at the Red Cross Center in the elementary school basement, rolling bandages, and when the tomatoes came on, they canned for The Woodford County Food Bank, never mind they knew absolutely nothing about the canning process. Most of their pretty jars of tomatoes exploded. Aunt Tott was still reeling from the shock of Uncle Freddy's untimely departure, and now, wouldn't you know, on top of everything else, both women were knee-deep in *the menopause*!

Tott sighed, "I just leave everything up to Pearl, especially now. Some days I don't know which end's up. It's just my luck to pick the hottest summer on record to have these flashes. They want to come on me with a vengeance. I can't get my breath and I soak right through whatever I have on, whew!" Pearl claimed Aunt Tott asked for trouble in the heat. "You sure you want to wear that dress that binds you about the hips?" she mused as Tott crossed the kitchen to the refrigerator. She could just make out Pearl's muttering above the hiss of steam spewing from a pot of boiling crabapples. It was Pearl's day to put up the pale crabapple jelly. She had picked a scorcher to stand over the hot stove, but she was quick to pass judgment on Tott's powder-blue linen dress. "Trussed up like a Christmas turkey and going to sit up most of the afternoon at a bridge table in this heat, but it's none of mine to say." Tott was due for bridge at two o'clock at Buck Pond and but for the electric fans and high ceilings out there, the humidity could very well claim all eight of the duplicate players.

The pot spewed more sweet steam into the heavy air and Pearl shot an eye to Tott, who was dabbing at herself with a little lace hankie. "Miss Tott, that poor little scrap of lace couldn't mop a tear," she muttered. Dear Tott had already worked herself into a sweat just getting the pitcher of ice water from refrigerator. She poured a tumbler full. "Ninety-five if it's a degree," she sighed and pressed the damp cloth to her breast, rolling back her eyes as if she had suffered another piece of sad news. Her hairdo from Razor's Beauty Shop had fallen flat and a few sodden wisps clung tight to her forehead. The powder-blue linen dress did have a tight hold on her. "It hikes itself up in the back because it can't find its way past your hips," Pearl informed her.

Lord love her, Tott was weary. She was all too aware that her mature bulk now exceeded her size-ten dress. The insufferable heat brought on flashes all during the night and she whimpered, "I can hardly remember when I've had a real good night's sleep." She spent nights flinging back the sheet one minute and then yanking it up again along with the counterpane after she cooled down, still damp from the flash. Pure and simple, she was having a hard time of it. But she wasn't the only one. Pearl, these days, would just as soon throw a plate across the kitchen as to look at you. She kept a couple of big white handkerchiefs in her apron pocket to mop at the beads of perspiration she swore were the size of early June peas that sprung onto her forehead and jumped off her into the fiery kitchen air. Even in the middle of winter she fanned and sighed and took herself out on any porch that was handy to cool down in twenty degrees. Pearl said it could not get cold enough for her. "Zero degrees is not one bit too cold for me! And the sultry summer is my trial by fire."

"I will not have you calling me a trussed-up turkey or whatever you muttered over that steaming pot of yours and I have decided to go upstairs and change into my green dress, no thanks to you," Tott said, fleeing the kitchen heat and Pearl's pot of crabapples. She paused in the doorway, looking downright hurt. "You know as well as I'm standing here, that was a *mean, mean* thing for you to say. My feelings run *as thin as tissue paper* in this heat. How would you like it if I talked to you that way?" she asked and went fanning down the hall.

Regardless of the season and despite sweltering Kentucky summers, my mother and the Aunties each put their best foot forward every day of their lives whether they felt up to it or not. They were powdered and dressed each morning at their breakfast tables, they changed before noon if they were scheduled for bridge or a luncheon, bathed and napped in late afternoon, and dressed again for suppers prepared by Pearl or Eva Belle Twyman. I witnessed all of their determined struggles with a girdle, and all in the name of beauty.

The old maid Taylor sisters displayed hats, purses, and gloves in the front window of The Style Shop facing onto Main Street, but they offered foundations in the back of the shop by the side of the courthouse and the jail. The Playtex Panty Girdle came tightly rolled inside a slender, pink cardboard tube with simple instructions: *Apply talcum powder to inside of Playtex Panty*

Girdle, roll girdle down, and step in. But no amount of powder could help the girls pull on the pink rubber horror in the humid Kentucky weather.

It was every bit of thirty minutes later when I came into Pearl's steaming kitchen and she told me, "Miss Tott, she needs to take herself out of here for the bridge at two o'clock and it's past one-thirty now. You run upstairs and bring her on down." She handed me a corn cake left over from lunch and I made my way down the long hall, up the curved stairs, and back to dear Tott's bedroom. Nothing I had ever seen could have prepared me for the sight of my aunt heaving and tugging at her Playtex Panty Girdle. It clung fast to her and water issued freely from every pore of her body. Sallie Gay and Sudie always said Tott had a natural blush and that blush had ripened to scarlet. She saw me standing there in the doorway but was unable to utter one word. She had rolled down the girdle in order to get a good grip on the slick rubber but she lost her hold on the piece and it slapped back on her to raise a welt the size of her pretty hand. "Don't you tell," she gasped with what little breath she could muster. "Not one word of this to anybody! God forbid, to your mother or Sudie Louisa, for God's sake. It's their fault I'm in this fix. They wear these hellish things and I wish for all the world I had never seen one!"

She was purple in the face. "Run get me a glass of ice water, honey," she moaned as she tried to lower herself down on the hassock at the foot of her bed to rest, but the rubber stuck fast to her hips, tight as a second skin, and she was so bound up she was unable to sit. As I turned to rush for help and ice water, I heard her mumble, "I'm just glad my Freddy isn't here to see this." I was afraid she had gone down like our milk cows when they bloated up, foundered on alfalfa, and when they went down... they never got up again. I did as I was told and left her there to fetch Pearl and the ice water, racing back down the long hall, slipping on summer rugs, down the spiral staircase, yelling all the way out into the kitchen, "Pearl, Pearl!" and all the time wishing that hellish Playtex Panty Girdle had stayed rolled up in its tube on the shelf in The Style Shop where it belonged. "She's down, she's soaking wet, and she needs water," I blurted out. "Sweet Jesus Lord, *help* us! I knew it," Pearl declared. "She's working with that rubber girdle again!"

My aunt didn't give a thought to her expanding waistline or to squeezing herself into that *foundation* when Uncle Freddy was alive. That man loved every inch of Tott. He would have cut that pink rubber horror into thin strips and found a good use for it in the garden. I might do that and have plenty left over for slingshots too. The goddess *Beauty* had my generous, storytelling Aunt Tott hogtied in the summer heat.

Beauty compelled my talented mother to sit before her mirrors applying powder and paints. Whom did *she* strive to please? Was it the goddess or Doc, or the Buck Pond Bridge Club girls? Why did *she* need to please? Doc loved my mother with passionate abandon: he never scrutinized her eye shadow when he held her close and they kissed like there was no tomorrow. For decades, my Aunt Sudie Louisa had been held prisoner to hair dyes, nail polish, and nightmares of screaming, wild horses pawing the air around her. In a vain attempt to present the pretty blonde image she had been long ago, she worked on herself every day of her life. Who *was* my Aunt Sudie Louisa, if not a *Beauty?* I saw it as a curse, worse than Doc's temper, but I didn't have to choose the lesser of *those* two evils, and thank the Lord for that. I found beauty in other things, and I was born with one hell of a temper.

The Rabies

"MOST PONIES ARE MEAN AS HELL," Doc told me, "but when he nips at you, just let him feel your little riding whip on his ear and he'll act right." Doc chewed on a big Cuban cigar. I saddled the big pinto, Half Time, and when I pulled the girth tight, he laid his ears back flat and showed me his powerful grass-stained teeth. When I flicked him on the ear with that little leather crop, he took it as his signal to buck and rear. He nipped when I placed my boot in the stirrup. Even when I fed him, he shot out his hind hoof and bit at other horses twice his size. Joe said, "Could be he's got the rabies. I saw him kicking the *barn!*"

———

He snuggled sweetly and poked his nose into my pocket, looking for a sugar cube or an apple, and just when I thought everything was safe, he tried to bite my fingers. He bucked and reared and threw me over his head for a pastime and trotted back to the stable, leaving me lying on the grass with the breath knocked out of me. "Half the time, that Half Time's trying to kill the child!" Eva Belle declared. But I rode him and did a lot of my barn-smoking in his stall. My mother said I rode the mean pony just to worry everybody to death. "You have a nice little Shetland pony and that sweet old mare you unfortunately named for your Aunt Sudie Louisa. I can tell you right now *that* did not set well with Sudie, the very idea of calling that old mare Hot Flash. *For – ever – more...*"

I was almost seven years old. I could drive the tractor, ride the setter, and set tobacco "Good as Zack!" I had no intention of riding a sawed-off Shetland. That was for babies, and poor Hot Flash was so pigeon-toed that Joe said, "The old roan has to pay one hoof a nickel to let the other one pass." Somebody needed to get on the good side of the hellion. It was going to be me or I would die trying.

One afternoon, after dropping his hay down from the loft, I eased myself down into the hayrack and lit up a Lucky Strike butt. The second he saw the toe of my boot protruding through the bars, he pushed his muzzle right through the hay and clamped his big yellow teeth onto my foot like a vise. The spiteful pinto aimed to bite off my toes. I tried to kick him away with my other foot but he laid back those ears and held on. I screamed and kept on screaming. I threw the lit cigarette into his face and the sparks and screams caused the mean-as-hell pony to slowly release my foot and to back off, shaking his head.

I managed to wriggle the toes—at least they were still there— but my foot was on fire. The Lucky Strike was a cold butt on the stall floor. I was as limp as his halter hanging on the hook. I could barely see for my tears to climb back up to the loft and then down the ladder to his stall, but I was determined to give the Pinto a taste of his own medicine for a change. With my foot swelling fast inside my tight boot, I clambered into his stall, finding him wild-eyed and prancing on the straw to show how mean and powerful he was. I lunged at him, threw my arm around his neck, clenched a fist full of mane, and gripped his ear in my right hand. In spite of his twisting and turning and angry snorts, I hung on, and then in one bold move, I bit right through that piece of hide, grinding my big teeth through his ear until my strength gave out. I released my grip and slid to the ground, spitting, and mopping at my face. My mouth was filled with pony hair and blood. He looked a little stunned.

I hobbled from his stall leaving him to toss his mean head from side to side and began my hike from the barn to the house and to Eva Belle. I hopped and dragged myself to the back steps and yelled for help. At the sight of my face smeared with dirt, tears, and blood, "What now!" she cried. "What have you gone and done this time, baby? Where does it hurt? Let me see your mouth. Have you knocked a tooth out?" She searched my face and dabbed at the blood with her apron. "It's not my face; it's my toes, my toes. He bit off my toes and I can't get the boot off." "You and that wild pony of yours, omph! Stand up here and let me see." She helped me to stand on one foot. "Thank the Lord your daddy's home." Together we limped up the back steps, through the porch, and into the kitchen where at last she sat me down, propped my leg on the low kitchen stool, and then slowly pulled at the boot. My toes and half of the foot had already turned blue.

She lowered her head and took my hands in hers. "Be still, be still," she whispered and held on tight. "You listen to me now, and you listen good." Her eyes were moist; she had that worried look I knew so well. "You *cannot* continue to behave like this, baby. Like your mother says, you will cripple yourself or worse." Now Eva Belle was down on me for doing something that seemed so natural; the son of a bitch pony bit me first! She was disappointed and frightened, pleading with me just like Sallie Gay to change my ways. "Nobody understands why you do these dangerous, wild things." She cocked her head to one side and asked, "Tell Eva Belle the truth, baby. Is it that you can't help yourself?" It was too much for me. I couldn't bear to ever be without Eva Belle and Joe Collins. What *was* wrong with me? Where could I go? What would become of me? I wailed louder.

Doc and Joe heard the racket from the study and hurried through the swinging door. "Jesus H., what in the world?" I tuned-up my crying again, not so much from the pain, now that the boot was off, but from the trauma of my wrestling match with that mean-as-hell pinto pony that stood every bit of fifteen hands tall and the awful fear of being orphaned by Eva Belle and Joe Collins.

Doc knelt before the wounded foot. "What in God's name happened to you?" "He bit off my toes," I sobbed. "Lord a' mercy, what a sight," Joe muttered, and hurried off to the study to fetch Doc's black medical bag. Eva Belle patted my dirty hands and fretted, "If that thing isn't busy running off with you, he's busy throwing you to the ground to knock the breath from you, and now he's come after your foot." Doc was looking closely at the foot. "He fixed you good this time, didn't he now? Your mother might be right. I believe something *is* wrong with that pony." He came at the blue foot with alcohol and gauze and I lunged halfway out of my chair, shielding my toes, "Don't - you – TOUCH – the - foot!" I screamed, wagging a finger in his face. "Don't touch the foot. You'll kill me if you even touch it." But he bribed me with running-board riding and a new pony if I would allow him to treat the injury. Joe repeated over and over, "That wild pony, I declare, I believe he's got the rabies." Joe Collins was *forever* talking about the rabies. Doc had once told him about a man who ran the Texaco gas station in Millville, who was bitten by a mad dog, and when he finally got to Doc's office he was foaming at the mouth just like the dog. They shot the dog but I never knew what they did with the gas station man.

At last a little calm settled over the scene as Doc delicately wrapped my foot and secured it with a metal clamp. "It's only a bruise, honey. Looks a lot worse than it is." He held my foot carefully in his hand and whispered, "You're brave, baby." I drew myself up as straight as I could in the chair and looked him squarely in the eye, almost nose to nose, and I thought to myself,

You don't know just how brave I really am. "I bit the mean son of a bitch back," I told him. He looked like a startled fawn and then, slowly, a broad grin spread from ear to ear. "Did you now? Bit him back, did you? By God, you're Doc's little girl alright." Joe shook his head: "Little Pig, you won't do."

Doc carried me out to the sunroom where the bridge club usually met and placed me on a lounge under the paddle fan. He propped my burning foot up on pillows and told me, "Be perfectly still until I come back, shut your eyes, and relax like a good girl." Joe handed me a glass of ice water and together they left the room. It wasn't so bad all alone out there under the cool breeze, beside me a large bowl of pink snapdragons and baby's breath. The pain eased a little. Most likely, they were all in the kitchen puzzling over *this* adventure. When they cooled down, I would promise to be good.

A few days after I bit the pony, Doc came home for lunch. It was rare that he left the office in the middle of the day. The Buck Pond luncheon ladies chattered on the sun porch as they were served a summer dessert of egg kisses and lemon sherbet to fortify them for a demanding afternoon of duplicate bridge. He paused at the screened door and gazed at Sallie Gay. He looked as if he might cry. She was lost in conversation, her dark head tilted to one side. He slowly opened the door, moved directly to her, and touched her shoulder as if she sat alone. She placed her hand on his, raised her green eyes and smiled. "I think I'll take a nap in the hammock," he said. He took my hand and we made our way past the card tables, nodding and speaking to the Buck

Pond girls, and finally down the wide front steps. "That handsome man," I heard them whisper. I followed him outside onto the lawn and watched him stretch out, relaxed in the hammock. What a fine sweet moment. He held out his hand and moved to make room for me beside him. I climbed onto the large swing Doc had designed. Abraham Foreacre, the carpenter, had bent wooden slats and bound them together with hemp rope and the result was a swinging bridge, gently curved up on the sides to hold us. I settled in next to Doc and crossed my right foot over my left ankle as he had done. He pulled his arm around me and I reached up to get a firm grip on his thumb. "Daddy's little girl," he said. His eyes were shut. My small world: It was just fine.

Toddy Time

TWO DAYS LATER, we were preparing for Doc's birthday party on July 25th. Gifts were already wrapped and placed in the hall for the party the following evening. The front hallway stretched thirty feet, with rugs scattered over the uneven random-width floorboards. An octagonal English rent table was usually piled with letters, car keys, gloves, and often a bowl of cut flowers. Beneath dark primitive oil paintings, a pair of black Hitchcock chairs flanked a drop-leaf table. It was a peaceful, dimly lit room, especially on early summer mornings, hushed as Sallie Gay, carrying her flower basket and shears and wearing a wide-brimmed straw hat, strolled out to her garden, and as Doc picked up his black-leather bag and set out to make hospital rounds. One by one we went striding past the deep bass *donk, donk* of the grandfather clock at the foot of the stairs, that majestic old clock that watched us come and go. But the sweet serenity of our front hall veiled the commotion that blew through the front door without a moment's warning to run rough-shod over Persian rugs, past the bowl of flowers and the tall clock.

Eva Belle had already planned the menu. I wrapped my present in white tissue paper, tied it with the brown and yellow grosgrain ribbons I used to hold my braids, and hid it in the kitchen pantry behind the Mott's Applesauce. I prayed Doc would ask if I had a present for him so I could race to the pantry, snatch it from behind the Mott's, and hand over the green-marble fountain pen holder. The Rexall druggist gave it to me because it was cracked right down the middle, but you couldn't see the crack if you tried.

It was that special time of day they called "toddy time." Sallie Gay and Doc sat a few feet from me on the breezy porch, rocking in white wicker chairs; he was sipping his bourbon. I was curled up in the swing on soft green pillows that smelled moldy after a rain or in the early mornings when they were still cool and moist with dew. The paddle fan moved heavy humid air, cicadas in the old maple trees hissed like chicken frying, and doves on the gravel driveway seemed to plea for rain.

The lazy drone of summer sounds was shattered with his outburst: "Jesus H. Christ, it's hot!" Doc drained his glass and rose to fix a sweetener. "Tobacco crop has dried up in the fields," he growled, as if the heat spell had knowingly done him an injustice. "And it's just now the middle of goddamned July." He was sweating and chewing hard on the cigar in the corner of his mouth. "I'll tell you right now..." His voice was rising and the silver jigger with his father's initials, *RMHH*, trembled in his hand as he poured his drink. "It's a worthless crop, worthless, and all thanks to your goddamned FDR, Franklin Rooosahvelt, who wouldn't know a government support price if it was looking him right in the face."

He jerked a wilted handkerchief from his pocket, pressed it hard to his eyes, and for an instant I thought he was crying. He rubbed it over his prominent forehead and ran his fingers through his thick blonde hair. With a silk necktie tight at his neck, a deep flush to his face, suddenly he looked too weary to fight his own anger. "Christ, it's hot as a July firecracker," he exploded and took off on President Roosevelt again. "I wouldn't give you a plug nickel for a man who sashays around in an opera cape like one of my Bantam roosters!"

He never changed his tune about FDR and Eleanor, and he harped on the same things over and over. He rattled the ice in his toddy and gnawed at the cigar while Sallie Gay rocked impassively. She looked fresh and cool, tilted her head in his direction, and with a tone that chided him, said, "I don't believe the President, or Ellahnoah either, for that matter, has much to do with the weather." Flirting with his anger, when his face was blood-red and he was already in a swivet over FDR or the weather, was like waving a red flag in front of a bull. Surely she knew it, knew only too well there was a white heat inside him.

———

"No one can talk to you," she said. He returned to his chair and sat with a heavy groan. I knew he was swearing again but I didn't listen. I stared up at the big hooks in the porch ceiling and wondered how they could hang down yet hold up the heavy swing. He slammed down his glass, spilling most of it on the straw rug, and lunged from his seat. His chair continued its rocking. The switch had been thrown. It could have been the slightest change in her tone or a glance shot between them that provoked the fury. Anything could trip his hair-trigger temper. She stared up at him, and in one motion rose to her feet, too, and scolded, "I can't talk to you, no one can talk to you when you are like this." She hurried into the house and he quickly followed.

Did they forget me? I scrambled out of the swing and stepped into the hall, watching as he stood in his study before the desk. He slammed the drawer shut. He had the pistol. I bolted through the house to my safe place, to the kitchen, to Eva Belle, Joe, and Sallie Gay, screaming for them all the way down the long hall, past the birthday presents, the grandfather clock, into the back hall, past the breakfast room, and finally into Eva Belle's kitchen. I reached the tall swinging door and pushed through it to find all three of them, but Doc was just one step behind me and he threw back that heavy door with such force I thought it might crack against the wall.

His mouth was twisted, his lips trembled, and the vein pulsed in his high forehead. A little piece of tobacco clung pitifully to his lower lip where the cigar had been just minutes ago. "The gun,"

Sallie Gay cried, her frantic eyes stared at him above manicured hands she pressed to her mouth. He raised the gleaming revolver with the pearl handle and pointed it directly at her face. He fixed his pale blue eyes on hers as he eased back the hammer. Eva Belle took me by the shoulders and scooted me to the far side of her kitchen. "Hush, hush now, don't you say one word, *not one!*" Joe stepped forward, pleading, "Doc, you know you don't want to hurt anybody." Joe moved slowly toward the man he had known most all his life. "Doc," he whispered. "Don't, Doc." He stared at Joe and looked as if he might burst with the rage. "I'll show you who's crazy, I'll show all of you!" he bellowed as his right hand flew out and he slammed the pistol hard against Joe's mouth. His wild eyes searched the kitchen walls and our faces; his broad shoulders heaved beneath the soaked shirt. He spun around and left the room.

I broke free of Eva Belle and ran to Joe, who knelt on one knee, gripping the corner of the marble table to steady himself. He covered his bleeding mouth with the other hand as if he had said something wrong. Eva Belle hurried to him with wet towels. "He's the meanest white man alive," she repeated over and over. Sallie Gay kept both hands to her face. Her eyes were shut. She sighed as she slowly moved through the kitchen door, to go where, I didn't know. Eva Belle set the tea towels down on the table where only yesterday we made cookies and rolled beaten biscuits. She took Joe's face in her hands. "Look up here to me now, look up here and let me see to your mouth." She spoke to him in her stern manner, but when he raised his head, her body sagged at the sight of him. She cradled his bloody face to her starched white apron and rocked him. "Now, now, look what he's gone and done," and her anger came on strong. "Look what that wild man has done, to you of all people!" She made Joe look right at her. "Nobody did one thing to that fit-throwing hellion, least of all, you."

I held on to Joe's arm so tight I pinched his flesh while I dabbed at my own tears with my shirttail. Eva Belle pressed the cold cloths to his wound but blood poured from his mouth and drenched the towels. It ran down his neck and soaked the worn collar of his blue work shirt. He was half crying and fighting hard to get his breath but he grabbed my hand and looked at me hard. "It's alright, Pig," he whispered. "It's alright, baby, its over."

Joe and Eva Belle knew Doc through and through. I knew they pitied him. They pitied all of us but we never talked about that, we just tried to weather the fits and let things cool down. After a time, our kitchen would be calm again and filled with the fragrance of her cooking.

Sometimes after supper in the evening, before Joe drove Eva Belle home, they worried over Doc or retold his antics. "We been weeding the tobacco all week long—Zack, Little Rabbit, and me—and when I looked up right before dinner time, here he came, running that big automobile across a field of cattle, full of cows and calves." Joe poured a dab of cream in his coffee cup and lit up a Lucky. "We figured he might tear the belly away from that La Salle, but he yanked it to a halt next to the patch and jumped away from it while its motor was still going." Joe rolled the cigarette between his fingers, gently touching its embers to the side of the ashtray, shutting one eye and tilting his head to avoid a curl of blue smoke. "He whipped around the three of us for a bit, then by grab, he laid into us, laid into Little Rabbit who never did a thing to nobody. Old man Greene came out from the County Agent's office to look at a piece of hail damage about that time and he laid into him."

Eva Belle stepped over to the table and held up her palm as if to say, stop. "Old Forrester was doing that talking." Joe shook his head back and forth, "No, Ma'am, he was stone-cold sober. Finally wore himself out I guess because he took that car right back across the pasture and out the front gate, pitching gravel ever which way, crazy acting." "Crazy?" Eva Belle said. "There's not a crazy bone in his body. No indeed, just mean. I wish I had a nickel for all the times he's gone and thrown a fit at me then tried to fire me to boot. Make you swimmy-headed to count."

Joe tried hard to dismiss Doc's shadow side. "Guess I don't pay Doc much mind, to tell you the truth." He sighed and made a graceful motion with his hand as if he was waving away a fly. "Let it all blow over, he don't mean it, let it pass, take him for what he is." "You can let it pass if you're of a mind to," said Eva Belle, "but someday, somebody will hold his hand to the fire! You make light of it if you want, but I'm here to tell you, that man's come into my kitchen for the very last time to rant and rave. You mark my words: he'll go just like old man RM, throwing a temper fit." Joe said, "He takes spells, just let it pass, like you say: 'Leave it lay where Jesus threw it.'" "Sweet Jesus wants no part of this business," she declared.

Like my hellion granddaddy, Doc woke some mornings just itching for a good fight. No one knew why. I slept on the sleeping porch directly above the breakfast room in the summertime and I usually woke to the sweet smell of apples frying, the thick fumes of coffee percolating, and bacon simmering in a black cast-iron skillet, or to the window shade's touch against the sill and the easy slap of the screened door out on the back porch. In the sunny breakfast room beneath me, bay windows faced the morning light, china cabinets with glass doors covered the walls, and the counter held pitchers of orange or tomato juice, small pitchers of milk and heavy cream, hot breads, the bacon, eggs, and the pot of coffee. A table-for-four stood in the middle of the room with a starched cloth and napkins rolled carefully in their rings.

One morning the door to his study slammed but I could still hear his muffled swearing. Drawers opened and slammed shut—the day too new for his anger. Did he wake in the night in this rage? Who could have said something wrong at this hour? Then Sallie Gay screamed, "Joe, Joe, come quick, he has the gun!" Eva Belle raced to the back porch; the screened door flew shut behind her as she called for Joe. I had never heard her raise her voice and now she wailed his name, "Joe, Joe, oh Lord, where are you?" But he was gone. Joe Collins was already in the fields or climbing onto John Deere, or out at Ocean Frog's store in Jacksontown buying a package of sweet Apple and picking up the hired men. What in the world would happen to us without Joe Collins?

The French doors to the cozy breakfast room slammed shut. Sallie Gay was trapped with him and that pistol in the small room filled with sunlight, the counter brimming with Eva Belle's good breakfast. Their voices pushed up through the sleeping porch floor: his was sure and deadly; hers was pleading. "What has come over you?" Doc's cold threats and Eva Belle's lament for Joe came at me. I hid beneath the covers to pretend it was a dream. I waited for the shot to be fired, for my ears to ring with the report of a thirty-eight-caliber pistol. I saw the room below bathed in morning sun and blood. I knew this would happen someday; there had always been that unfired shot from the pistol with the pearl handle. I dug deeper beneath the sheets.

Eva Belle was beside me pulling at my covers. "Get up now, baby, I called the Sheriff, it'll be alright, he's coming." She tugged at the covers. "You get up and get dressed now for Eva Belle." She meant business. She helped me into my clothes as she might dress a dummy in The Style Shop window, moving my arms through starched sleeves and hurriedly making my braids without brushing my hair. "No time for that," she whispered to herself, "no time."

She took me by the hand; she was going to lead me down the back stairs to the scene in the breakfast room. Why? Why must I see it? Why couldn't the two of us run down the wide front stairs to find Joe and then out the front door and away? But her strong, cold hand held tight to mine. As we silently crept down the steps, I tried to bend my knees so I wouldn't fall, but my legs and the toes in my brown shoes were numb. Had she laced them too tight? The numbness climbed up my legs, a loud ringing filled my ears, I couldn't breathe, I couldn't speak, and I couldn't hear. I lowered my useless stumbling feet, desperate not to fall or make one single sound. We reached the door at the foot of the stairs and stopped at the sound of voices.

Eva Belle took hold of the brass knob. She gripped my hand and her lips were drawn tight. She had to swallow hard to catch her breath. She didn't know what we would find. I couldn't hide and I couldn't run. I would see it. Slowly she turned the knob and together we stepped into the hallway directly across from the breakfast room. Sunshine filled the room as usual. Sallie Gay was seated in her chair, as usual, and Doc was handing the Sheriff a hot cup of coffee. "Sit right down here, Scooter." When they caught sight of me, they smiled and said, "Come to breakfast, honey." It could have been a dream or my imagination at work again, but why was the Sheriff sitting at the breakfast table?

Tobacco Cutting Time

"AUGUST IS THE LAST OF PEA-TIME and the first of frost," according to Joe Collins. "Tobacco cutting time," he would sing out, "let's hope the rain holds off." Men walk between the allless rows of full-grown plants six feet tall, and this time with machetes. They cut the stalks, carefully impale them on piercing metal spears, and then secure those stalks on tobacco sticks. The men bend, sweat, and slash with long broad blades sharp enough to sever fingers. If a man's not careful, or sweat sears his eyes to blind him for an instant, he can slit his wrist. If he slows midmorning in the heat or is half asleep and hung over from too much whiskey the night before, he can hack his ankle to the bone. Maybe he drinks to ease the pain in his back, across his shoulders, in his neck and down his arms; relieve a pain that sleep cannot hold back. Maybe he drinks to dream he won't climb onto the bed of the Grassy Springs farm truck out at Ocean Frog's store the next morning and the next morning and the next, next, next.

Within a few days of cutting, the exhausting work begins. Tons of yellow leaves are loaded high on wagons and truck beds and carried into the barns. Men roll up their sleeves, some strip off their shirts and tie bandannas or rags around their foreheads to fight back the sweat, and like circus acrobats, they thread their way up to the very top of the old barns where temperatures soar past one hundred degrees, maneuvering up the poplar beams, ten, twenty, thirty feet above the hard-packed dirt floor. They balance on slender rails at different levels, waiting to receive sticks heavy with leaves being handed up from the wagons below. The agile networking of lifting, handing off, and hanging continues through the long sweltering days until, finally, the last leaf is hung up to cure.

I can see Joe Collins standing in the long-legged shadows of my granddaddy's barns, beneath those rails and rails of dry golden leaves reaching up to the roof. I see him on raw November days, standing under tons of heavy moist leaves, and from Thanksgiving until Christmas, striking his pose again in the stripping rooms, his hands on his hips and the greasy old Stetson on the back of his head, listening to the men gossip beside warm coke stoves while the sleet blows wild outside.

Part Three

Pretty Things from Tots and Teens

THE AUNTIES WERE OFF AGAIN, heading down the road with their checkbooks to purchase my new fall clothes at Tots and Teens, shoes at Byck's as far away as Louisville, and they ordered from Best and Company in Chicago. Everyone knew my mother, Aunt Tott, and Aunt Sudie Louisa were style-setters. "We just *love* pretty things," they said.

They lived in gracious homes that held far too many rooms, some of which were shut off until holidays or funerals and in the wintertime: their heating bills were outrageous. Tott's garage still held Uncle Freddy's black Packard and his yellow Pontiac convertible with red-leather seats. To tend their gardens and lawns, to polish their brass and silver, and to maintain in general required a great deal of help, but those two women could not conceive of sharing one single inch of their space with each other. Doc called their extravagance "precious snobbery." Their homes reflected their good taste in fine English sideboards, Persian rugs, collections of luster pitchers, jade and malachite orbs. Doc swore, "They need to spend money on something every day. It's like a tonic to them! They spend money like it's water—on clothes, clothes, clothes—blazing up the road to that Tots and Teens Store."

They bought boxes of sheer white socks with scalloped-lace cuffs that slipped down into my shoe and formed wads under my arch before I could walk out the front door, stocked my chest of drawers and closet with more dotted-swiss blouses and sweet taffeta dresses, Belgian-lace blouses and yards of grosgrain and satin ribbons. I complained the dotted swiss brought on rashes but they continued to fill the closet with pretty things that itched. I returned the extravagant gifts to their fine boxes and hid them on the top shelf of my closet but, undaunted like water over stone, they spent money on pretty things.

Beauty

THE GIFT OF BEAUTY was confounding: its endless burden of responsibilities and the preparations required to maintain it. My mother's dressing table was covered with a mirror, a silver hand mirror rested face down, another large mirror hung above it, and a ruffled white organdy skirt hung to the floor. After her nap in the late afternoon while she bathed, I sat at her dressing table on the tufted pink hassock and listened to the music of Ira Gershwin or a waltz. The full blaze of the four o'clock sun struck my back and splashed onto the gold-framed mirror in front of me. Dazzling mirrors reflected more mirrors and illuminated the array of gold and silver. A porcelain bowl of white cotton balls and silver-backed combs and brushes glinted in the glass, and the mirrors reflected the pastel pinks and blues of Elizabeth Arden: fragile glass bottles, vials of colognes, lotions, and boxes of face powders. Slender gold cylinders of mascara and tiny pale pink containers of eye shadows for her green eyes. Tubes of lipstick and lipstick brushes, astringents, jars of cleansing creams, night creams, day creams.

Pale pinks and Blue Grass Cologne blues, it was an explosion of light, of colors, and the scent of her perfume. Rose-pink powder puffs, wispy and weightless, floated in a cobalt blue Dresden bowl. I closed my eyes and brushed one of the clouds across my face. It was her enchanted world. Did she eagerly sit before the reflections or was she helplessly caught in the spell of the goddess, drawn there by gleaming glass and gold? I did not know what lured my mother to faithfully come to this shrine, at its beck and call day or night, but I knew it took her away from me, far away from our times in flower beds, down on our knees in the dirt, calling each flower by name.

The goddess had no time for a sure-footed, one-eyed mule named Kate, my ragged dirty knees, or my greasy hat with dappled guinea hen feathers so beautiful to Joe Collins and to me. She was blind to the golden creatures weaving gauzy webs in my pony barn, unable to smell warm straw and mule sweat, afraid to recognize my courage to bite ponies and to set my tobacco plants. She had no time for the sharp taste of sweet Apple Chewing Tobacco. She turned the deaf ear to the rippling and trilling of granddaddy's ice-cold artesian spring and the magical tales Joe Collins plucked from the air.

Beauty lured my Sallie Gay away from waltzing with me in her bedroom to *The Blue Danube,* away from canning tomatoes at the Women's Hospital Auxiliary, away from designing old brick walks alongside her flower beds. I feared one day the goddess might claim her. I was frightened of *Beauty*'s power to hold my mother to her own reflection in that scrap of glass I could smash with the heel of my dusty ankle-boot—a dark glass that held her secrets in the night.

Poor Aunt Sudie,
Snowflake, and
Little Toad Tuttle

MY AUNT SUDIE LOUISA was named the prettiest girl in the Bluegrass by the *Sun* weekly newspaper in 1922. Decades later, that coveted article describing her golden curls and sparkling blue eyes still provided daily nourishment for her soul. "After all these years, that little piece from the *Sun* is still stuck in Sudie's craw," Doc mused. "When in God's name will it end?"

Aunt Sudie was the most offended by my appearance and she was the most vocal. "The child looks like an urchin from the Orphan's Home, or worse, like one of those dirty little things from the alley behind the filling station." Each morning Sallie Gay or Eva Belle brushed and braided my unruly shock of light hair and tied me up with pretty bows, but long before noontime the bows had flown off and I never replaced them. When Sudie Louisa got herself going on my peculiar style of beauty, that pink manicured hand flew to her breast as if another hot flash was coming on. "She runs around under that awful hat with dirty hen feathers and whenever she gets the chance she trails behind those mules, of all things, with Joe Collins, and she's up to *something* down in the cellar with those neighbor boys, too," she whispered as the eyes narrowed into a squint. "If she belonged to me, I would be looking into that cellar business, believe you me." Sudie never failed to add, "I'm here to tell you, no child of mine would ever be allowed to look that way."

Doc said, "There's a great deal of truth to what Sudie says since she has no children, and furthermore, if the Lord had seen fit to grant her issue, she would have powdered and painted the poor little devils and set them up on a shelf in the Chippendale corner cupboard where no dust could get at them. The Lord knew what He was doing there and I'll give Him credit for that one!" There was no way on the face of this earth I was ever going to be found sitting up on the shelf of Aunt Sudie Louisa's fine Chippendale corner cupboard. I planned to farm.

Doc warned, "Ginny Rae's Beauty Shoppe dyes and ammonia cold waves will eventually fry every living strand of hair from all their heads." Occasionally, Ginny Rae *did* hang too long on the telephone line while the color worked its magic. When the result was a bluish or pastel pink head, she didn't charge full price and she painted nails Arden Pink to match. Ginny Rae's was not the only salon in the town, but her popularity had soared since Miss Alma Tuttle's tragic episode with the ammonia cold-wave permanent at Razor's Beauty Shop, where solution was applied full strength and left on entirely too long with heartbreaking results. Just as Doc warned, ammonia singed most of the hair right off Alma's head. Her husband Hiram rushed her to Doc's office, where he prescribed sedatives for the both of them and treated Miss Alma's blistered scalp with ointments, to be applied regularly each week, with the head left uncovered to get the air. Aunt Sudie Louisa sighed, "Just lay me down to die if that ever happens to me. Everyone knows my hair is my crowning glory." Aunt Tott vowed to have herself done thereafter over in Lexington "in a professional salon." But loyal Sallie Gay said, "We should go right on back to Ginny Rae's where we belong." Their hearts ached for poor Alma. "She tries so hard to go on, bless her heart, just *bless her heart.*"

When Ginny Rae's Beauty Shoppe turned my Aunt Sudie's hair pink it put me in mind of our old mule Kate, who had a pinkish purple birthmark that started at the left nostril and ran all the way up her long face, through her bad eye that was stuck half open. I mentioned this one evening at the supper table and it caused Sudie Louisa to tune up and cry, but she cried at the drop of a hat. Doc said her crying was "just another one of Sudie's attention-getters." Sallie Gay said, "Your aunt is *beside* herself, just being mentioned in the same breath as that one-eyed mule, and rightly so I might add." "My bridge club girls still call me, Beauty, I'll have you know!" Sudie Louisa sobbed. And she was quick to add, "Beauty is one cross *you* will never have to bear or my name's not Sudie Louisa Harriss Holt Hall!" Although I named my barren old roan after Sudie Louisa, she was offended by that too, and thereafter never once asked about her namesake, Hot Flash. Doc was right; there was just no pleasing Sudie.

Everybody knew Sudie Louisa's first and only husband, Clinton Hall, ran off less than three years after they married, to hire on as a ranger working for the West Virginia State Parks. "Of all the godforsaken places to run to, just so he could get shed of Sudie," Doc declared. "Sitting up in a goddamned watchtower outside Elton, West Virginia. If that isn't the last of pea-time and the first of frost, you tell me what is. Sudie Louisa walked through the woods and picked up a broken reed when she found Clinton. He was never much force." But nobody blamed the man for leaving the hellcat Sudie, and Clinton never once failed to send a two-pound box of Whitman's Sampler to the family at Christmas.

After he high-tailed it off to West Virginia, Sudie stayed at our house for almost a year, claiming that a virtual army of doctors, lawyers, judges, and even policemen, wanted to force their intentions upon her. Doc said, "I suspect the only man in town to telephone Sudie in a year or more is Albert Potter down at the courthouse." He leaned back in his leather chair and laughed: "Seems sister failed to pay her property taxes, and after several notices came to her in the mail, poor Albert, the County Clerk, rang her up and asked if she could bring a check down." Doc laughed so hard he had to take off his tortoise-shell glasses and wipe his eyes. "Sudie says she knows exactly what Potter and the men who gathered outside the courthouse want from her. And what's more, she told me, 'I don't even walk on that side of the street anymore, so that should fix their kind!' Oh Lord, Lord, Lord, what is to become of Sudie Louisa?"

But even before poor Clinton fled, Sudie's delusions were flourishing, and she even managed to be insulted by the town's only Jewish shopkeeper, a small, well-mannered gentleman who owned the dry goods store. His shop was located midway between the Rexall Drug Store and Tootsie Sizemore's Sweet Shop down on Main Street, and early each morning, before the traffic started moving, he stepped through his front door with his broom and painstakingly swept the pavement all the way from his shop down to the drug store. Sudie's business with the druggist was concluded by eight-thirty that fresh summer morning and she set out for The Sweet Shop up the street.

The little shopkeeper rested his broom, bowed, and smiled at her, "Good morning to you, Missus." He said, "And how's your *Nubble* today?" "My *what?*" "Your *Nubble*, Missus, how's your *Nubble?*" he said again, smiling and drawing closer to her. She threw out her purse to fend off his vile advances as she staggered back toward the shelter of the drug store. "Police, police, help," she whimpered. The poor man's wife stepped into the street looking totally bewildered and wondering why her gray-haired husband was pursuing Missus Sudie down the Main Street with his broom. He caught up with Sudie Louisa as she blew through the front door of the Rexall Drug Store and into the arms of the pharmacist. She streaked for the safety of the prescription desk in the rear of the store, and the poor man sank into a chair at the nearest ice-cream table and tried to catch his breath. With trembling hands, he removed his gold-rimmed eyeglasses and pulled a handkerchief from his vest pocket. He dabbed at the perspiration that streamed into his eyes despite the cool morning, wiped his face, and began to wring the handkerchief in his hands. He shook his head back and forth pleading for someone to help him understand. "Oh, Missus, Missus, *Missus . . ."* he repeated over and over while the druggist ran to the telephone. "Central, get Doc and the police."

Within minutes, the shops on Main emptied into the street to form a lively parade. Customers poured out of The Sweet Shop with donuts and sweet rolls in their hand. The old maid Taylor sisters down at The Style Shop held hands and peeped through a crack in their door. Shopkeepers and the lecherous men who loitered in front of the courthouse hankering after Sudie Louisa and the boys from the pool hall stood chattering out on the sidewalk just like they did on December 7th, when the Japanese bombed Pearl Harbor! That evening, Doc had to administer a sedative, and Aunt Sudie had to be reminded of Clinton's membership in the Lodge in Lexington, where members were always respectfully addressed as *Noble.* "That tacky Lodge business," Doc said, "was typical of Clinton's need to belong to something, *anything* Sudie Louisa couldn't get her hands on. Poor ordinary son of a bitch runs around with a fez on his head and calls himself *Noble.* Deliver me."

Poor Sudie, she was always out of sorts about something or other. She was offended by the way people in the little town dressed or by their unfortunate deformities, and she took their innocent remarks to be insults. She had a way of silently clearing her throat and looking off to the left while she lovingly patted the pearls that hung loosely above her breastbone. "I just look the other way when I see that albino child they call Snowflake coming. If I don't run into him mopping the floor at the drug store, I have to look at him when we play cards at Edith's, where he works around the yard. Emile hired him to work in his chambers down at the courthouse, maybe because it's dark in the courthouse, and they say he can't tolerate the sun."

She was offended by the boy's appearance and she feared him, too. She was afraid of a frail little boy because he was different, because, to her, he was ugly and the child of mixed blood, because he was neither white nor black. She looked askance and wagged her forefinger back and forth: "He has no right to know my name, I don't mind telling you. 'How do you do, Miss Sudie,' he likes to say." She said it with a smirk. "He has no right knowing my name much less say it out loud and to my face."

Lord love him, the hapless child she took off on was only nine or ten years old and virtually an orphan. Joe Collins named him Snowflake. "That boy's neither fishes nor fouls, Pig. He's a palomino, you understand." Joe had a way of just slipping off the right word sometimes. It was a little confusing but I never said anything about it. Palomino is pretty close to albino.

Doc said he knew for a fact that the night watchman at Grissom's Lumberyard was the boy's father and his mother was a beautiful, bright young woman who worked as a nurse's aide in the hospital. He said, "The boy's father, LD, is worthless, but in many ways the bastard's brilliant. He can fix anything mechanical, any kind of motor, anything with moving parts, no matter how difficult. I believe he could fix my stethoscope or take the microscope in the office apart and put it back together blindfolded. Strangest thing I've ever seen, but he's a no-good, and there's no help there for Snowflake, I can tell you." Doc looked puzzled when he talked about the man's "lack of common sense" that relegated him to a night watchman's job while the weird and wonderful part of his brain ran like a fine Swiss clock. "What the hell," he mused, "I guess he's an idiot and a genius all at the same time. Regardless, the boy will spend his life sweeping floors and mowing lawns and trying to stay out of the sun, unless someone gives him a hand. It's just a shame; the child is as smart as a whip."

It never once occurred to me when I saw him sitting on the porch at Ocean Frog's store most mornings, with a grown man's hat pulled down over his pale eyes and dressed in a long-sleeved shirt, that he felt stuck tight between worlds of black and white, caught like the three-hundred-pound man who found himself trapped between the cold stone walls of Fat Man's Misery, a mile deep underground at Mammoth Cave. As I went inside to get my Orange Crush at Ocean Frog's, we smiled and spoke, but we never talked to each other like I talked to Ocean Frog or to Joe or to the hired men settling onto the truck bed. I never said more to him than "How you doing?" and he would say "Oh, fair, thanks." One morning as I waited for Joe out on Frog's porch, he offered me a stick of Juicy Fruit Chewing Gum. The fingers that held the package were long and tapered, freckled and pinkish, and the back of his smooth hand was rose-pink under the cuff of his blue work shirt. I reached for the stick of gum and looked up into his pastel eyes. He was smiling, his teeth were straight and white behind freckled lips, and he gently nodded his head. He had his mother's beauty and his daddy's peculiar brain. He swept floors for Ocean Frog in order to buy chewing gum, maybe an Orange Crush or an RC, and he offered that chewing gum to me.

Some years later, the men down at Ocean Frog's store would be calling him "Dr. Lewis Daniel Moore." Doc had cared enough to offer the bright young man a helping hand, and long after my daddy's death the letters continued to arrive regularly, first from his school in Ohio and then from the young doctor himself.

It took many years for Sudie's disposition to improve but improve it did. She actually mellowed in her sunset years, finally gave her hair a rest, letting it go gray and then white. She grew a bit plump, like a soft buxom quail, as did my dear Aunt Tott: plump little quails sitting in their white wicker rocking chairs on the broad porches or at the card table, laughing and gossiping, and still playing cards with a vengeance. I can see them now, patting their breasts and fanning with the score pad, leaving the roost to fan and stroll around a bit, and then, just like little feathered birds, flutter down again into their seats to resume their bidding. Perhaps it was the passage of time that took the edge off my Sudie's terrible disposition and gave her a trace of sentiment toward the last. Joe said, "Time can do that...if you *live* long enough." Aunt Tott called it "Sudie's benign retirement."

When she was about eighty, she met an orphan boy called Toad. "They called him Toad," Sudie told me, "called him that just for meanness, that poor little orphan thing and I'm here to say, the Orphan's Home people had no business farming out that child to strain himself in the Ice House, of all places, heaving fifty- or hundred-pound blocks of ice onto the back of the truck, then lugging them off again and into The Rexall Drug Store so everybody could sit back and enjoy a Co-Cola. I don't think even soaking wet he weighed more than one of those big blocks, and the poor frail thing worked all day long winter and summer, and then, if you can believe it, they sent him over to Floyd's Pool Hall to clean until ten o'clock at night. It made my heart *ache* to look into those eyes—eyes that said 'hungry for love,' and I know very well why the fat jailer adopted him. Your father always said the fat ones dig their graves with their teeth and he did just that, dropped dead at thirty-eight years old in front of the courthouse. Oh, to be thirty-eight again, just for a day. Well, that's what most of their kind do when they are on the public payroll. That jailer and his wife, Erline Hines, they grazed at the public trough like they both had a tapeworm. Anyway you look at it, they were as common as cat hair and couldn't wait to take in little Toad to do the cleaning in that nasty jailhouse. He would have been better off staying in the Orphan's Home, where at least he could have a hot meal and a nice clean bed."

My childless Aunt Sudie adopted little Toad Tuttle and loved him in her mind, but it was late, more than fifty years too late. It was at this time that Sudie's oscillating electric fan began to play well-known Episcopal hymns. As the hymns droned in the background, she fingered her string of pearls and smiled. She liked to sing along and many times I found her happily seated by the remarkable Anglican fan, humming along and remembering the plight of that sad little boy called Toad. "Fairest Lord Je-ee-sus, fairer than the meh-eh-dows, hum dah dah dah and the mor-ning sun. Je-ee-sus is fair-er-er, Jee-sus is bri-hite-ter than all the dah da heaven can boast."

Old Crows!

TWO YEARS LATER, WHEN I WAS NINE, Doc suffered a severe coronary that would have killed most men. When I heard Joe tap at the door of my fifth-grade classroom that September morning, I knew something terrible had happened. Sister Josephine opened the door and I saw him mopping sweat from his face as he strained to tell her quickly why he had come. "His heart..." he stammered. I sprung from my little green desk chair as Sister hurried back to me, her pale gray habit swirling around her shoulders. She placed my hand in Joe's. We ran down the brick path and out to the car stopped in the middle of the street, its motor still running. "He's in bad shape, Pig. Fighting to breathe."

He spun the car around and we roared off down the Pike in first gear—the La Salle's big engine whining and straining. Joe threw it up into second gear and held it there. He clinched his bandanna in his left hand and held it to the ivory steering wheel, staring straight ahead as if he were driving our road for the first time and didn't know his way. "I'm afraid he's gone, baby, gone," he cried. It could be a mistake: there was no heart attack I prayed. But as we flew through the front gate and into the driveway, pitching brown river-gravel in every direction, we found the police car and the town's only ambulance from the funeral home parked in front of the house. Joe's two brothers, dressed in overalls, stood silently under the tall porte cachre, and somewhere out on the lawn, by the flower beds, their mowers and leaf rakes and garden hoes lay right where they left them when Joe called for help.

Eva Belle hurried down the front steps with her arms open. "Come quick, baby, he wants you right now." She grabbed my hand and we ran up the wide stone steps. "You come, too," she yelled back over her shoulder to Joe. "Come on! Come quick!" The three of us raced through the front door and down the long hall. I stumbled through the door to his study to find Doc lying on the floor, gripping Sallie Gay's hand, a black rubber oxygen mask covering half his face. The oxygen tank hissed; smells of alcohol and panic filled the room. I knelt on the floor beside them and she gave him my hand. "She's here, Doc." Eva Belle gently cradled the back of my head and whispered, "Tell him you love him, honey. He tried to wait for you."

—————

Stretched out on the floor by his desk, he was fighting hard for each breath. How could this happen to the big man who wore big hats, smoked big Cuban cigars, carried a big mahogany walking stick with a carved handle, and had a passion for big cars, a man with his collection of shotguns mounted behind glass doors in the case by his desk, a thirty-eight revolver with a pearl handle in his desk drawer, and a lead blackjack covered in soft leather in the glove compartment of his big silver automobile.

Now he lay flat on his back, gripping my hand, as Sallie Gay and Joe Collins hovered over him. He was frightened and crying; his high forehead was pale and cold to my touch; and his thick hair streaked with gray was wringing-wet. Streams of sweat ran back through his sideburns into his ears and soaked the pillow beneath his handsome head. He struggled beneath the mask as the stretcher was brought into the room and those keen, deep blue eyes—always so sure—flooded with panic. Joe rose and nodded to the ambulance driver to relinquish the stretcher. He leaned over Doc and whispered in his ear, his voice a high-pitched whine, "I'll lift you to the stretcher my own self." Doc put himself into Joe's hands and closed his eyes for the first time. Joe placed his arms beneath Doc's back and neck and, in one slow powerful motion, slipped him onto the stretcher as gently as he set hens back on their straw nests. "I got you," he said in that whine. They carried him outside and loaded him into the back of the ambulance for the ride to Saint Joseph's Hospital, twelve miles away in Lexington. Doc was unconscious but Joe whispered to him again, "I'm coming right along behind in the La Salle."

To the amazement of his fellow physicians, Doc survived. In a couple of weeks, he felt well enough to make a few demands: "Get this goddamned useless bed out of here, hook up the oxygen so I can get my breath, and tell that poor excuse for a cook I will not eat this tasteless food. I'll have my meals prepared at home and Joe can bring them to me." The Catholic Sisters infuriated him. "Bunch of old black crows," he called them, and they did resemble black birds nodding and bobbing their hooded heads up and down, carefully pecking at suet with seeds. They floated up and down the marble corridors and in and out of sickrooms as if they were riding on air waves; their soft black-leather soles touched the floor but made no sound while the chatty, starched nurses slapped along the halls in large white oxfords, telling jokes and waking sick people to see if they were asleep. Doc held court for a month in Saint Joseph's, with baskets and trays of food delivered daily until his personal larder occupied most of the space in the refrigerator on his wing. He entertained with a well-stocked bar at toddy time and then was finally sent back home to run himself ragged again. Despite his strong constitution, there would be no recovery, only an unrelenting decline.

Haint Blue

CLOCKS TOOK THE PULSE of our home and laid down our rhythms. The big polished-metal kitchen clock kept time silently, but the fine old grandfather clock at the end of the front hall sounded rich clangs every fifteen minutes and chimed long sonorous gongs on the hour. The second hand of the ornately carved clock on the mantel in Doc's study produced a continuous *did-not, did-not,* and rang thin bells on the hour and half-hour. The Bulova watch strapped to Doc's wrist by a soft brown-leather band scampered like a jackrabbit when I put my ear to it: *sip-sip, sip-sip.* As surely as my father Doc took a patient's pulse with one hand and counted the heartbeats with his *sip-sip* Bulova, our clocks and watches read the pulse of our house.

171

After the heart attack, Doc constantly worried about his health. He took his own pulse several times a day. He closed his eyes, put the stethoscope to his heart, and frowned as if he never heard there any news that pleased him. He maintained a running dialogue with cardiologists at the Mayo Clinic and Johns Hopkins Hospital, where the doctors forced him to cut back his office hours. He was already making fewer hospital rounds and had given up entirely bird-hunting and the all-night poker games.

In early September, after lunch one Saturday, as he left for the barber shop, Doc said, "Be ready at four o'clock and I'll take you to the new farm." I ran alongside his car. "Just us?" I asked. "Just the two of us?" "Just the two of us," he said, lighting his cigar, and then he was through the gate, onto the road. For some unknown reason, he bought five hundred acres at auction in adjacent Anderson County, where the land was so poor it could only grow what Joe called Christmas tree cedars. "A cedar can grow itself on a rock. They can't grow a good enough corn crop in Anderson county to have a decent dove-shoot." Doc had a hard time resisting an auction, especially when a piece of land or farm equipment was being sold off on the courthouse steps for failure to pay taxes. "I picked this one up for a song," he liked to boast, but when he took a second, and certainly, a third look, he often found it was worth exactly what he paid for it. For a pastime, he bought and sold farms and houses, hay balers, tractors, and horse trailers. He just didn't know what to do with himself.

Though Anderson County sat adjacent to our county, we were separated by a yawning gorge with the Kentucky River running through it, and once you crossed over the long bridge at Tyrone you found rock and the cedars, hog farms, and poor crops. But Doc claimed the new farm had one saving grace: a Civil War home that was big enough to hold half of Lawrenceburg, the county seat of Anderson. "It's in bad shape, I grant you, but it was magnificent in its day. However, its day came and went about a hundred years ago." Joe saw the old house with Doc right after the auction and he didn't care to go back. He said Doc bought a pig in a poke and he knew for a fact the place was haunted. "The front door's painted Haint Blue." He rolled his eyes and shook like a chill had run up his spine. "A Haint Blue door's there for one reason and one reason alone, to keep the spirits out." He rolled his eyes back until only the whites showed and whispered, "The ... bridge ... at ... Tyrooone." I opened my eyes wide as saucers, stretched my mouth across my face like a skull, and trembled, "Tyrooone, Tyrooone." I had a nightmare about a bridge hanging over black rushing water in a bottomless gorge.

I could hardly wait until four o'clock when we would drive across the treacherous bridge at Tyrone, and maybe he would let me steer the car or ride on the running board back a shadowy lane to the Haint Blue house. They said narrow ice-covered roads wound down, down, down to the bridge from both sides and trucks loaded with tobacco, cattle, and horses spun out of control and were hurled over the side. Cars with screaming passengers, whirled round and round, slammed into the cliffs, and were thrown back again through the concrete guardrail and into the awful silence of a last, long, deadly fall. I saw the cars tumbling end-over-end in slow motion, plunging into the dark river, and then slowly, finally settling on the dim bottom, or hanging upside down, caught in the branches of an old tree ripped from the banks by a wild spring storm. When it was possible, they sent tow trucks down the steep banks to drag the river, but in the middle of winter, that was impossible. Violent spring rains produced raging currents that swept cars and trucks downriver and washed rusted metal and pitiful remains close to the shore. Even Doc, who feared nothing, admitted, "The bridge at Tyrone is a death wish in the icy wintertime." But it was not yet winter and I would cross with Doc in the big silver La Salle.

He came home at three o'clock and went into his study to take a nap. When the grandfather clock at the foot of the stairs finally said ten till four, I raced upstairs to retie my braids. Doc wouldn't care about dirty hands and knees so I let that go. Back down the stairs as the old clock gonged four times, down the long hall past the dark portraits, and into his study, ready to go. He was asleep. He usually stretched out on the big leather sofa directly under the paddle fan, but now he was sprawled in his reading chair as if he had fallen back. His arm hung over the side of the chair. The pain medication he was to take every four hours and an empty glass were still in his hand. He knew better than to mix Old Forrester and pills. His red-and-green-striped necktie was loose at the neck and his face was as red as the silk tie.

The Swiss clock on the mantel began its harsh tinny four o'clock bell-ringing. He never moved. When I leaned down to take the glass from his hand, the Bulova was racing, *sip-sip, sip-sip, sip-sip,* in sync with the clock on the mantel, *did-not, did-not,* and with his heavy breathing. A blue vein throbbed on his forehead and the monogram on his shirt jerked with every heartbeat: JPHH, *sip-sip, did-not, did-not,* JPHH, *sip-sip, did-not.* Twenty minutes past four. We were not going to the Haint Blue house.

Suddenly he choked and coughed. He opened his eyes and looked at me, but he was dazed and still half asleep. "Fix me a sweetener," he mumbled, and then waving his hand back and forth and shaking his head from side to side, "No...do it myself." He was on his feet, running his fingers through his hair and clearing his throat, trying to rouse himself. He took the glass from me and moved across the room to the dark mahogany whiskey-chest and slowly opened the double doors wide. He stood before the amber bottles of bourbon, polished jiggers, and silver ice bucket as a high priest stands before the altar. I grew up at this altar: julep cups and jiggers were polished sterling, decanters were crystal and dressed with silver chains dangling loose around their necks like the pearls above my Aunt Sudie Louisa's breastbone. With great care he selected a fresh glass, a larger one, poured his bourbon, and dropped in a cube of ice. "Let's go to the farm before it gets too late," he said, still facing the altar that held his sacraments.

The clock in the hall struck on the half-hour as we went out the front door. Thirty minutes past four. We climbed onto the La Salle's soft gray upholstered seats, drove through the gate, and breezed down the road. Just as I'd hoped, when we had gone a few miles, he let me steer. He rested one hand loosely on the wheel and sipped his drink with the other one. We were on our way to see Haint Blue after all. He talked about the old house, the people who lived there, and how they lost the place for failure to pay taxes. We began our winding descent down through the cliffs, rounded a bend, and before us, far below, loomed the bridge at Tyrone with the narrow Kentucky River snaking beneath it. The steep banks of Anderson County, dotted with Christmas tree cedars, stood waiting on the far side. I took my hands off that ivory steering wheel like it was a hot potato, and he directed our slow descent. Solid limestone and shale cliffs passed within five feet of my window, and every now and then, fragments of mica glinted and little waterfalls spilled from the stone walls as we eased our way down to the bridge. We were the only car crossing and there were rowboats and fishermen far beneath us upstream as we crossed. Why had I feared the bridge at Tyrone?

Doc steamed up the winding hill in Anderson County and I resumed my steering. "A little past five," he said as we pulled up to crumbled columns, weeds as tall as young trees, and a gate that hung from one rusted hinge. "This is it," he muttered, looking as if he might reconsider this purchase right on the spot. "Well...we'll see," he added. The avenue leading back to the house was choked with more weeds and bushes but the big La Salle rolled over it while he cursed, "Poor white trash."

The road was almost impassable; the Civil War house defied description. Most of the columns gave up the ghost long ago, leaving the second-floor porch in the same perilous position as the front gate: hanging by a thread. Shutters dangled beside a few windows and some of the panes upstairs were broken out. The whole building leaned to one side, making the battered roof look like a cocked hat.

He blasted the thunderous horn three or four times. "Where in the hell is what's-his-name?" He leaned on the horn again, and they came from the house and the vegetable garden: a thin man and his wife and four children ranging in age from two to twelve, all of them dressed, as Sallie Gay would say, from the beggar's press. The thin man's shirt and overalls hung on him like rags on a tobacco stick. His dark red hair was long and wild, his brows were bushy, and his eyes were a startling robin's-egg blue. A dirty apron covered the woman's dress. She straightened the apron and fidgeted with her hair, pulling back the loose strands, tucking them behind her ears. She was young and plump and blonde and tired. Dry vines and weeds hung from the porch roof. Their garden was already dying and picked to the bone. What would the place look like in two months, in bare November's gray cold light? "Edward *something*, that's his name!" Doc snapped. "Don't remember his last name, doesn't matter, Edward's enough for *him*." He winced, rubbed his left arm and his chest; he took a leather-covered flask from the glove compartment and swallowed two more pills with bourbon. He stepped out of the car and hailed the man by the wrong name. "Ho, Ned, just came to look around the house again." With a quick nod he dismissed the man's wife and completely ignored the children, contrary to the little people who came to his office for a needle in their behinds and took away a quarter for their pain.

The thin man and his family looked so small beside the sleek silver automobile, and the man was dwarfed standing next to Doc. That auction on the courthouse steps took everything he possessed, everything but his family, who stepped back as one to let Doc pass as if the King of England had come to call. For all we knew, this farm had been in the man's family since the house was built in 1866. It was possible the man's granddaddy built this fine house while RM was putting up his first poplar tobacco barns. Where would they go and how could they bear to lose their land? Doc and Joe said, "If you have land, you can make it, you can always raise a field of potatoes."

"Afternoon, Doctor," he said. "Yes, yes indeed, please come in, but mind where you step in the house, a lot of boards gone." He turned to me and smiled hello. "We have a daughter about your age." He had few teeth and he wasn't a day over forty. "I'm ten," I said, "but I'm little." Doc spoke too loud and laughed too much as we walked up to the porch. "Take a quick look," he sang out, and then slurred his words a little, "b'fore Yankees come back." The thin man and his wife flinched. No one had to tell them the place was falling down and strangled with weeds. I had never seen this side of Doc. I flinched at the tone he used, this big man with a red face and cigar.

We stepped onto the porch and I found myself face to face before the luminous blue door. So many years have passed and I still wonder what daring ran through their veins, prompting them to paint the massive door Haint Blue. The proud blue entrance turned a deaf ear to bare-bones poverty and kicked a little sand in the faces of those who might come with a big Cuban cigar and an expensive silver automobile, its gleaming metal figure with outstretched wings poised for flight on the hood. I imagined a fine craftsman, a Confederate soldier making his way back home after the war, who stopped to admire the Georgian-style house, and who stayed on for months etching exquisite patterns in the wood. Whoever he was, when he set out again on his long walk to Natchez, he left his heart and soul in that magnificent door.

The empty entrance hall was in shambles. Our footsteps and voices ricocheted off the high ceiling, off the deep hand-carved woodwork and the walls, where heavy faded paper dangled in long thin strips, waving in the slight breeze. Doc chewed on his dark cigar as he strutted forward. When he marched through the paneled double doors leading into the dining room, his right foot shot straight through a rotten floorboard. "Jesus H.!" he roared and down he went. His tortoise-shell glasses skittered across the floor. The man and his wife rushed to him, but he was unconscious, his leg wedged tight through the planks up past the knee.

How in the world would they free this big man, what were his injuries, why was he unconscious, did he hit his head? The oldest boy was quick to tell me, "We don't have a telephone anymore." His mother began to wring her apron, and her husband, slowly moving his head from side to side, knelt beside Doc. I prayed this was another bad dream, and I suddenly realized I could not call Joe Collins. With one leg under him and the other caught in the trap, Doc looked uncomfortable but he didn't seem to notice: he was limp as a rag. With a nod from her mother, one of the younger children picked up the eyeglasses and handed them to me. Doc didn't notice when the man, his wife, and two of the boys took hold of him to slowly heave his dead weight off their floor. It was well after seven o'clock when they managed to half carry him onto the front porch, down the uneven brick walk, and set him into the car.

They settled him carefully on the soft gray seat. He was slumped there in the car just as he was in his study a few hours past. The man loosened the striped tie, the blue vein bulged again, and the monogram resumed its jerking: JPHH, *sip-sip-sip,* JPHH. His mouth hung open wide; a continuous stream of dribble ran through the deep cleft in his chin and onto his fine shirt; he belched. Just as the man's wife leaned into the car to place a pillow from her porch chair beneath his head, Doc soaked the thick upholstered seat and his linen trousers. Urine coursed down the leg of his pants, drenched his sock, and puddled on the floorboard.

These children never once saw their father like we were seeing mine. The man's wife put her hand on my shoulder and for the first time she smiled. She had a caring smile and straight, white teeth. I was grateful for her touch. I was scared and ashamed, but if they could paint their door Haint Blue, I could drive the big car home. I would listen to Joe Collins and somehow he would get us there.

You drive that La Salle like you run ol' John Deere, Pig. Give
it a little gas and let up easy on the clutch.

But I could barely reach the gas pedal and see the road through the big ivory steering wheel. If I had to drive in the dark, where was the light switch, how did I shift the gears? Would we be caught on the bridge at Tyrone in the pitch-black dark? Where was Joe Collins? Was he lighting up a Lucky under the old crabapple tree, or sitting at the marble-top kitchen table stirring a little dab of heavy cream in his coffee?

Let me at those big teeth. If I can't work a kitchen match loose
from Pig's front teeth, then my name's not Joe Collins!

The thin man turned on the headlights, just in case, started the car, put it in second gear, and kept his foot on the clutch while I climbed in behind the wheel. But I put my foot down too hard on the gas and the car lunged away from him, leaping forward. My heavy door slammed shut, we lurched around the overgrown driveway, and roared back down the avenue over weeds and wild honeysuckle bushes.

The way that pony of yours bucks and roars, I swear I believe
he's got the rabies!

Doc pitched forward and then slammed back against his seat, the worn out porch-pillow landed in the pool of urine, and I turned onto the road praying it was the way home. I set my course down the middle of the narrow pavement, wondering what I would do if someone came from the other direction. Tears scalded my eyes before I knew it, running down my face and into my mouth. My whining and crying caught me by surprise.

Half Time is a good name for that pony. Half time he's tolerable and half time he's throwing you to the ground. Get back on, Pig, and show him who's boss!

Maybe Joe was on his way to the bridge. My fingers felt frozen to the wheel, I couldn't wipe my eyes, and what little I saw through the steering wheel was a blur. I didn't know if the car had gas, didn't know how to start it up again if it decided to stop, and I couldn't push the brake with enough force to bring it to a halt anyway. Maybe Joe was around the next hill waiting for us in the farm truck. He would load us up and head for home before it was dark on the bridge. But the truck wasn't waiting over that hill or the next hill or around curve after curve, so I played a game: Joe *was* waiting for me, but he was just out of sight.

It was darker now and the lights began to glow on the dashboard. Doc never moved a muscle. You could have cut the thick smell of bourbon and urine with a butcher knife, but I couldn't roll down the windows. We inched around a tight curve, still riding the black line in the middle of the road, and without any warning, I saw it, the bridge at Tyrone waiting below. I took my foot off the gas pedal and prayed the big car would stop. Joe was sure to be parked at the other end of the bridge, but I couldn't make out the truck because the tears kept coming on their own. It was darker now. We slowed. I could let the car stop and sit there until Doc woke—sit there all night if we had to. It would be better than crossing the bridge in the dark, but I couldn't stop the car. I let my eyes dart to his chest. Were his initials keeping time with his heart and his *sip-sip* Bulova watch? It was a relief to hear his snoring. Still straddling the black line, and in the middle of the bridge, I kept my eyes on the road and looked for Joe.

Always be glad they gave you your grandmother's name, Anna. She was the strong one.

The headlights were brighter and a blur, everything was a blur. A tire might blow, the car would turn on its own to crash through the guardrail, and Doc would never know—he would never hear me scream. I wouldn't scream. I was too scared to scream.

"Everybody has a pretty lunch box but me." Well, you're not just everbody, are you, Pig?

We finally inched to the other side and I began my crawl up the steep hill by the little waterfalls in the limestone cliffs. It was dark but we might make it home. The tears stopped just as they had started, on their own, and I shouted as loud as I could, "Doc, wake up!" I yelled his name over and over but he never heard me. The black line on the pavement disappeared so I guessed at the middle of the narrow road as I prowled around curves, up and over the hills.

You got to pay Mister Piper, too, little Pig.

The headlights shot through the dark to tell Joe we were coming and to warn cars and trucks we were heading straight down the middle. Gauges and dials on the dashboard glowed brighter, the big engine hummed, Doc's breathing was deep and regular, and I was still listening to Joe Collins as we pulled through the front gate and into the driveway. We were home.

You set tobacco good as Zack. Pig, you won't do!

I blew the earsplitting horn and they poured out of the house: first Joe and his brother Dan, who had stayed on just in case he was needed, Eva Belle with her hat on and ready to be carried home, and Sallie Gay right behind them. There I sat, behind the ivory steering wheel, with Doc out cold on the seat next to me. "What in the world?" my mother cried in a panic. Joe swore, "Good God amighty, Pig." And Eva Belle asked, "Is he sick? What in the world happened, baby?" When Joe opened the door and leaned inside, the stale cloud of bourbon and urine smacked him right between the eyes. He understood, and backed out of the car. He smiled and whispered to me, "How *you* doing, little Pig?"

The floodgates blew wide open again when he asked if I was alright, and without any warning my head bobbed up and down on its own, up and down, up and down, up and down, like a foolish wind-up toy. I couldn't stop my rocking and nodding. I stared straight ahead; I could not bear to look Joe Collins in the face. I would keep the Haint Blue trip to myself, hide it away with the old dry butts I still kept down in the tack room. Like that stale tobacco too strong to smoke, Haint Blue's bite was too bitter, but I knew I could cross any bridge anywhere, any time of day or in the middle of a pitch-black night. I was a bridge-crosser! I would find my way home, as long as Joe Collins waited over the next hill or around the curve.

They were all talking at once, and then they were gone to the house, having a to-do over Doc. Joe and Dan were undressing him, bathing him, putting him to bed. Sallie Gay and Eva Belle fussed over his soiled linen trousers. But I thought I might just sit for a time, behind the ivory steering wheel, in the big La Salle.

Heisey and the Hog

AUNT TOTT SAID, "I know I talk too much, I don't care if I do, your mother likes to say I talk too much. *You know our Tott, she talks a blue streak.* And Freddy used to brag, *My Tott can talk to a dead dog.* But I can't worry about that, I don't fret over those things anymore. There was a time when I stewed over everything in this world, right down to which straw hat to wear, and to tell you the truth I'm glad those days are gone. Those nagging, worrisome little things, the Fidgets, I called them, they thought they were so important, but it's as if they just packed themselves up one fine day and moved on while I was playing a hand of bridge. I never really knew when those Fidgets ran off to worry somebody else, and I'm here to tell you they had plenty of places to run to alright: everybody has the Fidgets now. Oh, well, I can't bother with all that."

Dear wonderfully long-winded Tott. I could tell she was primed and ready. I settled into a comfortable leather chair in front of the fire with my cup of tea and she didn't waste one second before she was at it again. "Bless her heart," she sighed, "I saw her last week down at the new C & D Market and I thought to myself, Haroldean does not look right to me. There is something about her that does - not - look – *right*. I believe I told your mother, and Pearl, too, she had a sort of, pallor, you know, her color wasn't right. Now she's gone, Lord love her, and I pray she's found some peace, more peace than she ever found with that Heisey. And, honey," she steamed on without a pause, "I believe I would like another cup of tea." I rose, took the cup and saucer from her. "Tea cakes, too, honey, you tell Pearl I said to *pile them on*. I haven't lost my appetite, I'm here to tell you." As I left the library, I heard her musing to herself, "Wonder what time it is, four o'clock, I'll bet you a nickel, every time I turn around it's four o'clock. Strange."

I knew Heisey McClain, well, knew him by sight, and what a sight he was. He didn't stand one inch over five feet tall and was as fat as a toad. Doc said, "Heisey's a half pint. *Let's Get Drunk and Be Somebody*, that's Heisey's motto. Umph, don't talk to me about little men and their big problems." The McClains were pretty important people in the bank, but the unfortunate Heisey Hightower McClain the Third couldn't hold down a job, not even at the family bank. He couldn't see over the teller's cage.

He lived off his wife's three, yes three, inheritances and drove the biggest automobiles he could get his hands on, propped himself up on a cushion so he could see through the steering wheel, and toured up and down the Main Street, wearing a French beret cocked over one eye. One time, drunk as a Lord, he ran a black Chrysler Imperial into the Big Sink when it was full of water and almost drowned. It was hard to pity him: the meanest little man in the town. Everybody knew his desperation to feel important drove his ugly-acting disposition. They all said Heisey was shallow as a plate.

I returned to Aunt Tott with a large tray: the teapot in its padded cozy, fresh napkins, a pretty plate of Pearl's tea cakes and finger sandwiches. "Lovely, just lovely, high tea and why not?" Tott beamed as she nibbled a thin slice of lemon. "We'll have these pretty little sandwiches now and you stay for dinner at seven and we'll have Pearl's pork roast with turnips and little buttermilk cornsticks." She was fortifying herself to run on about Haroldean and Heisey, and even before we took our high tea, she contemplated dinner.

"I suppose Heisey could be sweet if he wanted to, but when he took his drinks, well, Katy bar the door. You would not believe it if I told you some of the things that dreadful little man did, like the time it was almost zero with snow up to your knees. He started his drinking early in the morning and by early afternoon everybody on Elm Street had driven past his house and had a good look at his antics: he was busy pitching every piece of china and crystal Haroldean had to her name onto the driveway and he broke it all to smithereens, anything he could get his mean little fingers on while she cried and begged him to stop, bless her heart, and half the town passed by.

"Your father always said Heisey's automobile wreck permanently damaged him and that could very well be true, you know an injury to the head and all. It was that run-in with the hog out on the Clifton Pike. To hear him tell it, he was coming home from a meeting, at the courthouse of all places—well, that's where he *said* he had been—but I cannot imagine what business Heisey McClain had at nine o'clock at night in town, much less at the courthouse, most likely doing his drinking and lollygagging about in that dirty pool room behind the drug store. Oh well, whatever. He was in his sporty convertible and as he came around the tight bend by the old gristmill, down by the Glen's Creek Christian Church, he slammed into a full-grown hog. Struck it head-on, going forty miles an hour, and that little Ford flipped over two or three times, landing on its side in the Glen's Creek bed with its wheels still spinning and Heisey thrown downstream. Thank the Lord, little Harvey Lamb and his family happened to be carrying a load of young shoats to the stockyards that very next morning and they came upon Heisey in the creek bed. Do you think it's peculiar that Heisey hit a hog and a truckload of pigs found him? Well I do. Things happen for a reason, don't they? Always look for the significance, honey, in strange things.

"I remember when my Freddy hired the little Lamb man to do some work on the horse vans. He was fat as a hog himself, and he brought his wife along, Little Rosa he called her, and the two pudgy little boys, Kenny Ray and Roy Dale, who watched their daddy work and sang like little angels, a common bunch, but they did their best I suppose. They claimed they came from a place called, Pansy, Alabama, of all places. Do you believe there is such a place? Bound to be true, no one in their right mind could dream up a name like that. Alabama is somewhere around Mississippi, I think, and I would rather say I hailed from Alabama, wherever it is, any day of the week, than from across the Ohio River in Indiana where they say, *Take and put*. Well, whatever.

"I suspect it was all that Lamb man could do just to heave that battered unconscious Heisey into the back of his truck with the squealing pigs and it was just Heisey's luck those pigs had made a terrible mess in back of the machine that morning. It's something a hog is inclined to do, they say, a result of the nerves when they sense they're going to market. They're a lot smarter than we give them credit for, the hogs I mean. The little man took him to the hospital and your daddy sewed him up, stitched a four-inch piece of Heisey's brow back up to his hairline where it belonged, and set his broken leg as well as his wrist. His brow wanted to sag after that so he had a perpetual frown to match his disposition and he complained, from that day forward, of a tingling sensation in his left hand and that was peculiar too. The hand flipped like it had a life of its own. Isn't that odd? Think of it. Whipping around to a fare-thee-well outside the automobile window. Heisey was forever saying or doing something vulgar and that nasty hand twitching was just typical of him, believe you me. Eventually he just held on to the hand or kept it inside his coat pocket when he went to church, which was a rare occasion, let me tell you.

———

"Well, the Baptist preacher, Dr. Baker, lived right across the street and he walked over to Heisey's front gate and tried to talk some sense into that wild man, but Heisey threw cups and saucers at poor Dr. Baker, yelling at the top of his lungs, *Go do your mealy-mouthed preaching at the Baptist Church where you belong and get the hell out of my yard.* Now I've always liked poor old Dr. Baker. Lord knows, his own life's no bed of roses, his wife with that awful psoriasis—for all you know, she's has it everywhere—and there's something not quite right with one of the Baker children, I believe it's the one with red hair, it cannot sit still for love or money and it jabbers like a Polly parrot. It's no secret, Heisey and his whole family thought because they were Presbyterians, they were better than the poor old Baptists, and I must say, they do try to out-sing the whole town on Sunday, the Baptists, that is.

"As I said before, how Haroldean stood it I do not know. There was the time in the dead of winter when he took off every stitch of clothing and ran naked as a jaybird out the front door while she begged him to come back in before he caught his death. Of course, I would have locked and barred every last door and window in that ramshackle old house and the next morning little Boots McKinney the paperboy would have found an ugly icicle out in the front yard. That stunt almost killed him, too, gave him a good case of pneumonia that laid him out for a month while she waited on him, carrying heavy trays up and down, up and down the stairs. Yes, she was a remarkable woman to have put up with him. She must have been a saint. Or a sop, come to think of it. Makes you wonder. He's been dead a little over three years and I don't believe she was one bit happier without him, trudging into town in that dowdy old brown wool coat with a shopping bag over her arm, looking like somebody's washerwoman; makes your heart ache to think about it. You know, Haroldean had the saddest eyes to me. Like a sick bird, those awful, sad eyes set way back in dark sockets, she put me in mind of a sick little bird.

"Now you tell me. Why on God's earth did that woman refuse to drive the automobile to market? Heisey had bought himself a big green Buick with fluid drive, the biggest one they make, and drove it only one month before he died. But did you ever see her behind the wheel, did you ever see her, come to think of it, even riding, out for a drive, in that great big Buick with Heisey at the wheel? Not once. Not one single time did I ever see him take her to the grocery store in that new Buick of his. Now he's out of the way and there sits the car day in and day out locked up in the garage. Why didn't she telephone Mr. Redmond and have him pick her up in the taxicab? He could have waited outside the C & D to help with the packages, not that she bought enough to feed a bird. The grocery boys would have been happy to take her things out to the car and the taxi man could have seen her home and into the kitchen with her packages. But I can't worry about that now. Well, rest her little soul, that's where I last saw her, down at the C & D."

Ocean Frog's Store

For two days in late October, in order to entertain visiting Bishops and other holy people, Margaret Hall School dismissed the lower forms, the *little people* as we were known. Overjoyed, I grabbed a lunch pail and hopped into the farm truck beside Joe Collins. We breezed down the narrow road to pick up eight or ten farmhands in front of Ocean Frog's Grocery Store. Fall and early winter is the time to turn fields under, mend fencing again, prepare the stripping rooms, and see to winter-feed. The tobacco crop filled every rail in the barns, waiting for November rain and sleet to bring it into case, to make dry crumbling leaves moist and pliable for braiding into hands.

195

Now and then Joe sent a stream of tobacco juice flying out the window and sang out to a friend. "Hip Hop! How you doing? He's got what they call a clubfoot, Pig." The green truck pulled up in front of the little store plastered with tin signs:

Drink Dr Pepper 10 - 2 & 4
Chew Red Man
Sweeten Your Breath with Sen-Sen

Seated, as always, rain or shine, in every season, out on the front porch with a cool drink in his hand, was the dark fat man known to everybody as the Ocean Frog. "Drinking his Owenge Crush. That man and his cool drink, never seen him without it," Joe said, swinging open the truck door and greeting the men as he stepped off the running board. "How you this morning, Zack? Little chilly for that owenge drink of yours, ol' man Frog?" and "How you getting along, Yoke?"

Joe gave George Combs the name of Double Yoke. "Lord help that man's head, looking for all the world like he's got a double yolk! Yes, indeed, Jawage has a head the size of a ripe melon." In all his years of medical practice, Doc said he'd never seen such a head on a man. I slid across the seat and followed right along behind Joe, nodding to the men like he did. "Morning, Zack. Hey, Rabbit. Hido, Jawage." For love or money, I could not bring myself to say "Double Yoke," much less "Yoke," but sometimes I greeted him as "Mr. Yoke." I climbed up the steps and stopped in front of Ocean Frog's rocking chair. "Morning, Sir." Should I call him, Frog? Mr. Frog? He owned the store.

"Morning, Pig," he nodded. "You want your cold drink?" "I sure do," I told him and stepped inside his store to stand in front of the glass case as the worn-out screen door eased itself shut behind me.

There were a half-dozen holes in the flimsy screen, where Ocean Frog stuck little wads of cotton in the slits to keep out bugs, but the spring on the door had long ceased to pull it shut, so grasshoppers and crickets were free to rest in the shadowy corners and under the kegs of feed in Frog's place. Now the listless autumn flies sat on the screen, the light bulbs, the counter, ready to drop and be ground underfoot. Two small windows let in spots of early morning sunlight to scurry unsteady like little beetles across the floor. A few frayed hands of tobacco leaves dangled from the ceiling and I wondered if Joe brought Frog a few hands of prized leaves from last year's crop. They would probably hang there, shredding bit by bit onto the dusty floor until only a stem dangled from the ceiling, just like the flies that were dead and didn't even know it.

It was warm, close, and sweet smelling in the store. On the counter, Frog displayed tiny metal boxes of twopenny matches, Ex-Lax, Sen-Sen, and an assortment of snuff. Under glass, he had carefully laid braided twists of light leaves in a circle, and there were wooden boxes filled with Roi Tan Cigars, banded with fancy red-and-gold seals; packs of Lucky Strikes, Chesterfields, and Old Golds; but most of the space was reserved for chewing tobaccos: pouches of Red Man, Black Ambrosia, Plum Cake, Brown Mule, Southern Pride, and tightly wrapped light and dark chews, looking more like chocolate candies. I spied the cakes of Apple Chewing Tobacco:

Fresh — Juicy and Mild
"makes your mouth water"

"Aw, Pig! Get yourself ready to ride now," Joe called from the porch. Ocean Frog heaved himself up from the rocking chair and moved inside to the soft drink cooler. Winter and summer he kept a fifty-pound block of ice surrounded by a few bottles of Coca-Cola, Grapette, and Orange Crush in a washtub covered with a piece of old tarpaulin. "You want the owenge?" he asked. Nobody but Ocean Frog would sell me chewing tobacco and I knew the time to ask for it was now or never. But, would he? "What *else* you want?" he urged. "I think I want something right there in the case," I managed to mumble as the big man moved behind the counter, as Joe stepped inside and lit up a Lucky Strike and the hired men settled onto the truck bed. Their conversation and the soft clatter of lunch pails faded and the pounding of my heart took over, racing hard under the pink pig label of my Fink's overalls.

Ocean Frog raised the glass lid on the case and looked directly at me. His eyes were as big and round as the snapping-turtle eggs Joe kept in a tank out behind the henhouse, and were set so far apart they seemed to bulge from the sides of his dark head. I knew now why they called him Ocean Frog and I also knew I had to seize the moment. "I'll have the sweet Apple Chew today, please." My mouth was so dry I could have spit cotton. He removed the cake wrapped in red cellophane, waddled over to the metal strongbox he used as a cash register, and then waited for his stunned customer to follow. "Twenty-five cents for the Apple and a nickel for the owenge drink, less you got yesterday's bottle, then it's two cents back to you." I reached into the bib of my overalls and found only two dimes and four pennies. I was six cents short and just one jump ahead of a fit when Joe reached over my shoulder and handed the correct change to Frog. "Had myself a grape drink this time," he said and turned to leave. "Take your drink now and put the chew in your pocket." I tucked the sweet Apple in my bib and gazed at Ocean Frog. My eyes told him everything.

As the Grassy Springs farm truck pulled away from his store, the heavy man settled back down on the porch with his orange drink. He wagged his finger and hollered after us, "Aw, Miss Pig, your daddy know you chewing the sweet Apple Tobacca? I reckon that's ol' Joe's doings." I lunged halfway out the window, waved the package wrapped in red cellophane, and we were off to hitch up the old sledge behind the mules and eat our noon meal down by the ice-cold artesian spring.

Spit, Pig!

"I SUSPECT YOU *are* big enough to ride on the old sledge." We used the heavy sledge made of timbers as it was used in the time of my granddaddy: to smooth the earth after disks turned the field into rows of clods. It was hitched behind the sorrel mules, one-eyed Kate and faithful Beck, and weighted down with slabs of limestone the men lugged up from the creek bed. The mules paid no mind to the weight, maintaining a slow, steady gait as the crude beams ground the rich soil beneath us. It was a magic carpet ride to me but I couldn't see much except mules' tails and clods.

"Ground's looking fine as sugar, little Pig." Joe took both sets of reins in his left hand and removed his hat, wiped the pale bandanna across his face and over his bald head beaded with sweat, stuffed it into the hip pocket, and set the Stetson back on his head. It was Indian summer, a hot spell that comes in late October. He sent a little tobacco juice onto the next row and said without warning, "It's time for you to take ol' Kate's reins." He pressed the thick, dark leather strap into the palm of my left hand. My heart started up again beneath the Fink's and I felt myself go all "swimmy-headed," as Eva Belle called it. He pried open my right hand and laid Beck's reins between my rigid fingers. "Don't matter how much you pull on Beck, he'll do what old Kate says anyhow."

My hat was almost as big as the old washtub Ocean Frog used to cool his Grapette and Orange Crush, but I was grateful to hide in the sweet shade of the broad brim with feathers flying in every direction. I kept still but for my breathing. I suspect Joe Collins heard my wild heart racing that day behind the mules.

"Look up, Pig, let the mules know you got the reins." The sound of his voice jerked me back to grinding dirt and I realized the cantankerous one-eyed Kate might sense Joe had released his hold on her. She would be free to bolt and run wild, pulling old Beck along with her and dragging the two of us behind. I imagined our hats and the heavy stones flying from the sledge and Joe tumbling after them. But ol' Kate didn't have a care in this world who held her reins. If those two mighty mules ever took a notion to buck and run, there wasn't a farmer in the county who stood a chance of stopping them. They paid about as much attention to me as to the green flies that went for the bluegrass spittle around their lips. "It's your team now, little Pig; they'll work for you good as me."

I stood straight and tall, with the leather lines in my hands, and clucked to the mules as he did, "Gee up, Kate," and then again, "You come up here, now, Beck." I was too rigid to turn my head, to look up at him and smile, too tense to speak and almost too excited to breathe. My hands were streaked with dirt and the slick straps bulged between my small fingers. The earthy smell of mule sweat beneath heavy harness, the sweet fragrance of saddle soap, and the odor of Joe's chewing tobacco mixed with the scent of my own tension hung in the air above us while the old sledge kept to its course straight down the row. We moved in silence but for the mules' regular breathing, the squeaking and stretching of leather, and now and then a clinking, like tiny cymbals, of brass harness rings.

My fingers were numb by the time we reached the end of the last row. "Head on into the barn," Joe told me as he yelled up to the mule, "Aw, Kate, I bet your belly's so empty it thinks your throat's been cut." "All right, mules, you come up here," I sang out, and to my surprise, they turned at the fencerow. I swelled with pride. "You tell those mules, Pig," he chuckled and spit out his plug of tobacco. "Time for that wore out chew to go, wore out like me and these mules." I drove my team through the massive double doors and gratefully into the shade of the tobacco barn. Rays of late sunlight, swimming with a sea of life, shot through the open vents, and over our heads poplar beams reached forty feet high. "Ho, you old mules!" I hollered. My prissy little command broke the stillness. *Hooo mules . . . hooo mules* swirled and echoed up through the rails, disturbing the strange deep calm that settles over a tobacco barn in late afternoon or the hush that is caught lingering after dawn before the vents are opened to let in the world.

I brought the team to a halt and Joe eased the reins from my hands. He had no sooner stepped off that sledge than Kate shot out her hind leg at him. "Ho, Kate, you're a mean one! You stay a good piece away from her, Pig. She just as soon kick you up side your head as to look at you." We moved away from the team. He unhitched the heavy sledge and the mules gave a mighty shake beneath harness that rested lighter now over their broad backs. Their grateful shudder rolled like deep thunder on the heels of my command that ran thin as a silk thread through the barn, *Hooo mules, mules, mules.* Joe put his hands on his hips and arched his back. "Lord have mercy, I'm the oldest man I know for fifty-five, number-eight buckshot in my knees, and the *artheraetus* in my back." He winked. "I believe we need a little taste of the sweet Apple while old Kate cools down."

He reached into the front pocket of his bib, took out his penknife and the bar covered in red cellophane. With great care, he carved a sliver of the moist cake and solemnly looked down at me. His brow was knitted, his lips were pursed, the whites of his eyes were the color of the creamy coffee he sipped after supper in Eva Belle's kitchen: serious business. He lowered his dark head and spoke slowly. "Put the Apple under your upper lip and just suck on it ever now and then." My eyes never left his as I raised my hands to receive the communion of my first chew. I took the sliver from him and did as I was told. He cut a slice for himself, slipped it into his mouth, up and under the lip. My grandmother Anna and Richard Moses watched. Mules, emerald green flies, grasshoppers, gypsy people, and weary men in overalls with rags and bandannas tied around their heads gathered around us. The noble chorus that swelled in the Lyric picture show for Lash Larue rang from the old poplar beams.

Joe returned the paraphernalia to his pocket and in a few seconds it began: the tobacco burned like a red-hot fire. Its juices spewed onto my tongue, flirted with the back of my mouth, and trickled down my throat. I flapped my arms and whirled in circles. Joe's laughter scared the mules. Kate went wild, rolling her one good eye and kicking up a dust storm off the barn floor while poor Beck brayed and bucked. "Spit, Pig!" He yelled, "For Chrissakes, SPIT!"

It was on that afternoon that my spitting lessons began. Joe raised his eyebrows and worked the chew in his mouth as he studied my front teeth that now bucked well over my lower lip. "Pig, you got yourself a mouth just made for spitting. I'll have you sending tobacco three feet or more through those big front ones or my name's not Collins."

He chose targets within my shooting range. I took careful aim and let fly at cow pies, tin cans, and dead rats in the sheds until

I was able to land a direct hit on plump, green tobacco worms, butterflies, and the copper pennies he flipped onto the hard dirt floor of the barns. Before long I could spit at a moment's notice and strike targets as much as three and four feet away. His pride was unrestrained.

By Thanksgiving Day I held my first demonstration at high noon, out by Ocean Frog's porch, under the doubtful eyes of a half dozen men, most of who had chewed all their lives. Fat Daddy Rat Parrish, Jawage Combs, Little Rabbit, and Frog himself gathered around to watch at a respectful but amused distance as Joe announced, "I got little Pig out-spitting every one of you, by grab."

Joe flung his arms open wide, like a preacher at a tent-revival inviting sinners to come forth and take on Jesus, like the famous evangelist Aunt Tott remembered as a child. When protracted tent-meetings came to town, he whipped his congregation into such a lather, he had to send his disciples up and down the aisles between the chairs with washtubs to collect the money. "Let it fly, Pig, show these boys what you got."

Time for the exhibition didn't come one moment too soon; I had worked up a mouthful of tobacco juice. I nodded solemnly to Joe, leaned slowly forward, stretched my neck, and tipped back my head. I raised my right hand and pointed to a crumpled pack of Chesterfield cigarettes half buried in the dirt at least three feet away from the edge of Ocean Frog's porch. I heard the stifled chuckles behind me. I took a deep breath, calculated the arc and my distance to the target, and then drove my tongue into the back of those ivories with such force it shot a jigger of brown juice onto the Chesterfields. Joe slapped his leg and jabbed his finger into the faces on the porch. "Don't tell me that child can't out spit any one of you standing here. Don't she beat all?" They shook their heads back and forth and finally Ocean Frog said, "You won't do, little Miss, you just won't do."

The spitting business went a little sideways on me. I began to spit on anything and everything, with or without the sweet Apple up under my lip. It became a compulsion, a terrible tic. I made excuses to leave the room and trotted to the bathroom to spit. I left the porch to step around a corner out of sight to let fly. I could hardly pass up a fair-sized bug or bee or fallen blossom when Sallie Gay and I strolled beside her flower beds. I finally confided in Joe that I feared the spitting would become a curse. "Good Lord, Pig, that could send your momma and, God knows, your Aunt Sudie Louisa, to an early grave, or worse, give them the apoplexy. You do something about that: you whistle every time you want to spit." He puckered his mouth and knitted those brows of his as we stood under the old crabapple tree and worried together that I might go crazy with the spitting like cousin Dot Harriss.

I can honestly say I did everything I could to curtail the urge: I shook my right leg up and down so violently at the table that the china and crystal trembled, I gnawed on the inside of my jaw and I batted my eyes, as the spitting spawned tics and more tics. Sallie Gay and Aunt Sudie Louisa looked away when I shook and chewed and batted. If I even looked like I was ready to bat in front of the Buck Pond Duplicate Bridge Club, they were quick as lightning to say, "Run, honey, and get the phone." Aunt Sudie said, "At least it's not a sexual problem, the child's way too young for that, but something must be done!"

Just as Joe suggested, I began to whistle. I whistled entire songs and when I placed two fingers in my mouth and blew hard, you could hear the blast over in the next county. Thankfully, the call to whistle wasn't nearly as unbridled as my urge to spit. A few years later, they straightened my teeth with braces and more braces and rubber bands, and finally, a removable appliance, which made me lisp. They filed them down and polished them up. I kept the grosgrain ribbons tied in bows on the ends of my braids and wore sweet little skirts and blouses with Peter Pan collars. At last, Sallie Gay and the Aunties were pleased. I could shut my mouth, my teeth were straight, but I could no longer spit. Oh, maybe a few inches, if I pushed my tongue hard enough against the new formation, but mostly, the tobacco juice just dribbled down my chin and Joe had to look away.

The Grower's Market

ANYONE WILL TELL YOU there is no colder place in the middle of a Kentucky winter than the slab of frigid concrete at the tobacco market. Joe Collins and I stomped our numb feet, waiting for the graders slowly threading their way up and down the long corridors piled high with our baskets of tobacco. "Try to get a little circulation going, Pig." Joe looked twice his size, dressed in his Fink's over his long johns, two wool sweaters, and the plaid wool shirt I gave him for Christmas the year before, along with a greenish silk necktie with an iridescent peacock-feather design.

———

I bought the tie long before October and I didn't understand why The Graves Cox Store placed such a fine necktie on sale. Looking back on it, I am surprised my mother and Eva Belle let me give Joe that tacky opalescent piece of neckwear, but I seized the tie as soon as I spied it and thought it was the richest, grandest gift I could give him. I wrapped the Graves Cox Men's Store box in slick paper from the Rexall Drug Store, tied it with gold ribbons, and scrawled on the tag, "To Joe from Pig." I spent most of my Christmas money on that shirt and tie, with just enough left over to buy cookie cutters, a four-leaf clover, and a heart for Eva Belle. Mr. Archibald Bosworth, the bank manager, had sent a teller out to the house to deliver a red poinsettia, and I just happened to receive the delivery at the side door. I removed Mr. Atchie's card and replaced it, "To Doc from Pig." For my mother, I found an iron lamp on the dump by the railroad trestle. She had it wired, popped a pretty shade on it, and it stood on the porch by the swing for as long as I can remember. Eva Belle and I baked ginger cookies with the new cutters, Doc never thanked the bank for the flowers, and I didn't dream Joe would wear the iridescent greenish necktie with his red, yellow, and green plaid shirt, but he had it all on, plus his fine red suspenders, when he came in Christmas night for eggnog and he sure looked fine to me.

On the floor of the Grower's Market, he wore heavy boots and his gray wool hunting socks with a bright red band around the tops, a wool scarf wound around his neck, and the old hat set on the back of his head. What a pair we were, standing beside our crop. I was dressed in everything they were big enough to put on me in preparation for our tobacco sale days. I could hardly bend my arms for the long johns and sweaters layered underneath my coat and if Eva Belle could have slipped her hot-water bottles into the seat of my pants, she would have done that, too. It was a wonder I was allowed to go at all, but there I stood beneath a red beret, next to the big man in his Fink's. "We're a pair to draw to, little Pig," he whispered.

Despite Doc's declaration that he was the finest physician in the Bluegrass, I was sickly. Sallie Gay and Tott chose to say, "The little thing is *delicate*." In wintertime, I was forever coming down with the croup, which put me in the bed for tiresome days on end. On those gray leafless days my fireplace crackled; vaporous phantoms waited until dark and then leapt from the embers and across the ceiling, down through the flowers that papered my walls. Hot-water bottles wrapped in soft cotton jackets warmed my toes. Eva Belle and Sallie Gay smoothed Vicks VapoRub on my chest. Doc dispensed nasal drops and a vaporizer puffed and wheezed steam on the hearth. I gargled, I sniffed, and I ate clear watery soups and tapioca puddings. The cure was more exhausting than the cold and I only saw Joe Collins if he and Doc brought their toddies upstairs and sipped beside my fire.

The tobacco graders pulled a hand or two from the middle of our baskets, rubbed a piece of leaf briskly between their hands, and then breathed in the fragrance. I took myself a leaf, rubbed it between my bare hands until I felt heat from the shredded bits, doused my nose into my cupped hands and inhaled. Its peppery smell shot straight to my head like a rocket and it left a strong and bittersweet taste on my tongue. Buyers inched their way down the long aisles of burley, singing out their bids, "Seventy-four, five, six" and the auctioneer at the head of the line shouted, "Sold! Sold American! Sold RJR!" Our Grassy Springs leaves sold again and again to the big tobacco houses of Reynolds, Brown & Williamson, American, and British American. At last, half frozen, Joe and I waited close as we dared beside the potbellied stove in the Grower's office to collect our final checks, to be safely tucked along with the chewing tobacco in Joe's overalls pocket. How many more seasons would find him standing beside the crop, until every last scrap of it was finally sold? How many seasons already?

When the sales were finally over and Grassy Springs Farm had put thousands of pounds of leaves on the market, Doc and Joe leaned back in the leather armchairs, sipped bourbon by the fire, and talked big. "Best damn crop in the county, Doc, or my name's not Joe Collins!" Doc chewed on his dark Cuban cigar and crowed, "Hell, Collins, the best damn crop in the Bluegrass!" Those two big men took pride in the tobacco as they did in the Angus cattle, the mares and foals, even the sugar-cured hams and hot-sage sausage smoking in the smokehouse.

Right on the heels of the tobacco market, in the dead of winter came lambing and hog-killing time and I wasn't about to be left out. Joe Collins created a manger for the newborn lambs by sectioning off one entire end of a barn with heavy green tarpaulins used the month before to cover the tobacco as it rode to market. A dozen men carried supplies into the nursery: gallons of milk in shining metal cans to be heated on coke stoves, clean toweling for rubbing and swaddling stacked on crates, and fresh straw to be piled knee-deep. The men carefully ladled milk into dozens of RC Cola bottles and placed them in crates next to the coke stoves to stay warm. Dark men with plugs of tobacco tucked in their cheeks, dressed in wool caps, heavy overcoats, and long aprons that hung down to their ankles, with wool scarves wrapped around their heads and necks, hurried inside with lifeless babies, sometimes carrying two lambs under each arm. Throughout the long night they were nursemaids, settling themselves down near the glowing stoves and cooing to infant lambs. As the first few drops of warm milk trickled down their throats, the lambs came back to life and with each tiny first bleat I thought Joe Collins and his tobacco-chewing, cigar-smoking nursemaids were miracle-makers. Riding home before dawn with Doc and Joe in the La Salle, I wondered how baby lambs had survived before we fed them warm milk in Royal Crown Cola bottles from Ocean Frog's store out in Jacksontown.

Hog-killing! They would have to hogtie me to keep me from it. The weather had to be almost too cold to tolerate for fear the meat might spoil. Zack, Rabbit, and the fat man, Daddy Rat, set up sawhorses to support oak cutting-boards, which had been washed down with lye soap and scrubbed a hundred times until they were smooth and clean and the surface felt as soft as silk under my hand. Tiny lines creased the oak where years of razor-sharp knife blades sliced through raw meat. The icy morning light revealed steaming cauldrons, men moving silently, wrapped again in heavy wool, shuffling through patches of ice in thick-heeled boots. Cold steel blades slithered from their sheaths and were pressed against whining grinding wheels, sharpened to slash and slit the meat. Gray wisps of smoke puffed up from wood chips laid beneath the cook pots and knives caught the glint of early sun as Doc stepped from his car, dressed in a coat that fell almost to his boots, a fur hat pulled well down over his ears.

The Grassy Springs truck bounced and trembled as it rolled over hard frozen earth. A dozen rigid boars lay in close ranks on the bloody truck bed, their throats slit from ear to ear, eyes staring, bumping numbly against each other. It wasn't a pretty sight, but I wouldn't trade hog-killing time or nursing half-frozen lambs with an RC Cola bottle for all the dotted swiss and Belgian lace in this world.

Epilogue

WHEN I WAS SEVEN, I drifted through long seasons, with all the time in the world to imagine and wonder about anything and everything: about cousin Dot's spitting, Doc's rage, granddaddy's last frenzy in the cucumber patch—and what exactly *were* maggots, was it really possible the electric fan played Episcopal hymns only Aunt Sudie Louisa could hear, would I be a farmer like Joe Collins?

I began that summer as a butterfly dressed in a tutu and ended that glorious year chewing the sweet Apple and out-spitting Ocean Frog and even fat Daddy Rat Parrish. The years leap-frogged ahead to 1945 when President Harry S. Truman ordered atomic bombs named Fat Man and Little Boy dropped on the cities of Hiroshima and Nagasaki, the first Volkswagen Beetles were produced, Germany and the Imperial Empire of Japan surrendered. World War II ended. I had an uneasy feeling life was trying to move right out from under me. I turned around one day and I was ten, turned again and my daddy died.

I was right beside Doc when he died on Christmas Eve in 1947. The house sparkled with holiday sights and smells but he was in no holiday mood. He was too thin, too pale, too weak to sit beside the fire with his toddy and enjoy a good book or the tree that touched the ceiling. "I don't have the strength to open one goddamned Christmas present, not one of them," he said. He would never wear the silk ties and scarves and leather gloves, smoke the Cuban cigars, or drink the fine aged bourbon with parchment tags that read, *Made especially for JPHH*. "For God's sake," he said, "I'll never tie my shoelaces again."

Eva Belle baked for days in preparation, hoping to lure him to the table. Their entire lives had been intertwined, constant companions throughout childhood. He taught her to ride, they hid in cornfields and in the sunflower patch to shoot doves, operated on the barren sow, and after their surgical success, looked for anything sick or crippled to cut open and sew up again, planted their first vegetable garden, and Miss Lula taught them both to love cooking. Eva Belle knew why the doctors sent him home from the hospital, knew it the moment she saw his drawn face and the bony shoulders. He had not come home a moment too soon. She cooked everything bad for his heart and good for his soul: thick rich eggnog, a roasted goose, and whiskey-cake soaked with brandy. Throughout the day, delivery boys knocked at the back door with fresh flowers. Delicate hand-decorated candies arrived in gold boxes from the Lafayette Gallery Candy Shop, and as always, Aunt Sudie Louisa's one and only husband, Clinton, sent a box of Whitman's Sampler.

That evening, Doc's unseen enemy struck. "Oh, God!" he moaned, and Joe pushed past me and was onto the bed, rubbing Doc's chest with the full weight of his body behind every stroke. Doc's frail arm flung off the bed and shuddered under Joe's weight, his eyes and mouth opened wide, and for an eternity, he did not breathe. Sallie Gay laid her hand on Joe's arm and held it there. "He's gone," she whispered. "It's over." Eva Belle came into the room, "Oh, no," she whispered. Through it all, I never moved, I couldn't speak, and a loud ringing in my ears crowded out their voices.

Joe sat slumped on the bed and suddenly the silence exploded. Doc lunged straight up into Joe's arms, searching for air and drawing in his last gasp with a wail I would never forget. He pitched back onto the bed for the last time in Joe's arms. The violence of his dying filled the room and then rushed from it. We stood in a vacuum, too stunned to speak or think of our lives without him.

Visitors paraded in and out of the deep snow, leaving calling cards on silver trays. Two days after Christmas, we buried Doc. A line of black limousines crept into the circular driveway and snaked past rows of boxwood, so heavy with snow they resembled iced cupcakes that had dried and cracked open. I wore dark stockings, a navy blue coat with brass buttons, and in my pocket I carried the ten-dollar gold piece he gave me. The paths that wound through the cemetery were lined with faces peering in the windows at us. I pulled at my gloves and my tam and stared at the floor. At last the procession came to a halt and I stepped from the car to stand on the plot of ground that held most of my family since Civil War days. December wind shot streaks of dry snow slithering up the hill, away from the open grave. Relatives huddled in clumps under a heavy sky. I shut my eyes and listened to the crunch of boots, pretending for a moment I was riding on the running board while he steered the La Salle and smoked a dark Cuban cigar. Or it was summertime, late at night, and we were sitting on red-leather stools at the soda fountain, listening to the jukebox play Dorothy Shay's "Feudin' and Fightin'."

Joe pulled the scarf tighter around his neck. If Doc knew he was standing bareheaded in this snow and wind, he would most likely say, *Good god amighty, Collins, it's cold enough to freeze the balls off a brass monkey. Back up to this fire and take a little toddy to get the circulation going, a little tonic for what ails you at the end of the day.* I held my mother's hand as the funeral attendants led us down a narrow path to the large gray tent that slapped and flapped against the wind. Together we stepped forward with Joe to stand close to Doc. Her face was shielded from the cold, framed by her brown fur hood against the pale gray sky. With one hand I held tight to her, and deep in my pocket I clenched the gold coin in my gloved fist until my fingers were numb. Joe stood to my right and hard flecks of snow sat undisturbed on his round head. He cocked his head to one side and winked.

Clergy assembled by the coffin, cousins we had not seen for years piled into seats behind us, and the congregation that stood so patiently in the cold pressed forward to form a sea of faces on the open side of the tent. The wind pushed itself beneath the canvas, whipped it up and down, up and down, and swirled angrily around our feet. "I am the resurrection and the life, saith the Lord." The sickening odor of flowers and words for the burial of the dead rushed at me. "Ave Maria," cut through the air and I saw Doc listening and humming along behind his tortoise-shell glasses, that cigar in the corner of this mouth. "Ave Maria," a clear Christmas song for Doc, for those of us gone long ago, their headstones worn and nameless and covered with yellowed moss. I laid my hand on the bronze casket and let them lower him down to find some peace beside my grandmother Anna and Richard Moses Harriss Holt.

Late that afternoon I walked through the swinging door and into Eva Belle's kitchen as Little Rabbit teased Joe, "That necktie! It'll knock your eye out." Rabbit turned to Joe's brothers, "Where you think he got that tie?" "My Christmas from Pig," Joe told him. "When my time comes, I guess you can lay me out in this tie. Peacock feather, they call it," he added, as he fingered the iridescent design. "Don't talk to me about you being laid out; you'll outlive all of us. You got it easy," Rabbit told him. "He's always had the luck," he told the others.

It was a little past four in the afternoon and the crowd that followed the funeral procession back home had finally departed as new snow began to fall. The house was still except for waiters drying dishes and the vacuum cleaner running in the front of the house. Miss Ermine Grundy bundled up mounds of napkins, tablecloths, and tea towels and disappeared downstairs to her laundry. The men sat at the old marble table eating whiskey-cake and sipping coffee. They were uncomfortably dressed in starched white shirts, neckties at their throats under dark suits with buttoned vests, dark sheer socks, and wing-tipped shoes. Only a death would bring them in their three-piece suits to this table in the middle of the afternoon: Doc's death and Joe's need for them to stay close by. Joe fingered the tie then offered it up for them to see, "Come in a box with Graves Cox on it," he said in an effort to break the silence. "Most times I wore a necktie when Doc and I drove over to the Lafayette Hotel or to the hospital. I carried him away from this house for the last time this morning, didn't I?"

His hand slipped away from the tie and rested on the table beside his coffee cup. Eva Belle reached over his shoulder and took the uneaten plate of cake and brought him her beaten biscuits with sugar-cured ham. She touched his cup with a little hot coffee and stood quietly behind him. She placed her hand on his shoulder. He was trying to come to grips with things, so they left him to his thoughts. "I recall I was twelve, and that year was 1904 when we met, and I figured he'd be here long after we were all dead an gone. We are *old,* we're all way up there now but for you, Little Rabbit." "I feel old," Rabbit told them. Joe didn't hear. He gazed at the heavy snow settling on the window beside him, watched it cling to the warmth of the glass pane, melt and slip down to puddle on the sill. He knew in the morning there would be icicles.

The explosive times were buried with Doc; the temper tantrums were over, but he took too much with him. He carried away the flamboyant days of buying and selling properties and machinery, his unending projects, which ran the dizzying gamut from producing a better leaf of burley tobacco to curing the finest hickory-smoked hams in the Bluegrass. Before his heart failed, his unbridled energy allowed him to serve his passions and anything was possible in his world. "Paint life with a broad brush, by God," he commanded like my granddaddy before him. He took so much with him. The peace and calm that fell over us was as confusing as the turbulence he created.

Miss Spring rolled around again and in April, as always, Joe Collins and I ate some good rich dirt. I was fourteen. I danced around the Maypole. The school year drew to a close. Sallie Gay, Aunt Tott, and Aunt Sudie Louisa burst into their annual summer ritual and burned up the road shopping for me at The Loom and Needle, the newest and certainly the most fashionable shop for young ladies in the Bluegrass. Cotillion Club brought chiffon and organdy evening gowns, shoes with one-inch heels dyed to match, and boxes of white cotton gloves pouring into my closet. I replaced everything, except my riding clothes, with dresses, full skirts, blouses, and two-piece bathing suits. Will Middletown, the milky-eyed paperhanger painted the woodwork in my bedroom a soft white like whipped cream and papered the walls with pale yellow flowers. Aunt Sudie Louisa gave me her fine English dressing table complete with beauty instruments and, in keeping with family tradition, Elizabeth Arden geranium pinks and blue colognes. I let my pigtails down and took a good look at my blonde hair and straight teeth. It was as if I had been crowned, Princess Pig.

The boys rode their bicycles to the house and toted me anywhere I wanted to go, and sometimes we talked as if we had never met before. They opened a door for me, occasionally, and they excused themselves and went to the bathroom, and just when I thought I was really Princess Pig, they threw me into the pool fully dressed, or gave me their famous silent treatment because I refused to play football or mumbletypeg in the dirt. Lucie Cross and Trinette didn't seem so silly anymore and we began our years of all-night slumber parties, piled up on porch swings, tickling arms and giggling about boys until dawn. The Harriss girls and Aunt Sudie were ecstatic. Eva Belle told Joe, "I always said, once she got herself shed of that mouth full of wire, she might be a right pretty little thing."

At fourteen, I joined the ranks of the Upper School as a freshman and picked up a hockey stick for the first time. Sallie Gay played bridge, ran the Community Chest, and entertained with luncheons and small suppers for eight around her dining table. She was happier and more beautiful then I had ever seen her.

The days of bloody knees and biting my pony were behind us, and Sallie Gay made her first forays into the world of crops and barns and hired hands. Together we drove over the farms. I showed her our tobacco crop drying in the fields, the herd of Angus, and our flock of sheep. We stopped to watch hay being mowed and baled for winter, took a picnic lunch to the lake a mile from the road, and I proudly showed her the sections of pipe that carried water all the way from the lake to the tobacco fields. She was amazed at the scope of it and proud of me for my love of farming. At least one afternoon a week, Sallie Gay, Joe, and I met to go over farm accounts. I was excused from morning classes to go to the stockyards and in the winter to the Grower's Market.

That summer, my mother was admitted to Saint Joseph's Hospital in Lexington for tests, vowing there was nothing to be concerned about, but the examination and tests led to surgery. Sallie Gay met her diagnosis of cancer head on. She listened attentively, learned about her treatment and prognosis. She made a fair recovery from the surgery. By late summer, she felt well enough to think of flowers again, play a little bridge, and her appetite returned, thanks to Eva Belle's tomato aspics and chilled soups.

But I would not be consoled. I rode horses into a steamy lather, slammed tennis balls, swam laps, raced up and down the hockey field, and then ran to her for hope. Her humor and common sense carried even the most frightened of us along. It was the considered opinion of a dozen doctors from here to Baltimore and back that her condition was terminal, but she held a very different opinion.

One year later, she insisted, and so I packed my saddle and hockey stick and left for preparatory school in the Blue Ridge of Virginia. I returned for the holidays to find Joe Collins waiting at the airport—my mother, Aunt Tott, Aunt Sudie Louisa, and Eva Belle at home. We never questioned what miracles worked for us. As each Christmas rolled around, we raised our yule cups, drank a toast to her, and said a prayer for one more year.

Many times we returned to the hospital for treatments, but regardless of needles, tubes, and great discomfort, she asked for her pale pink Elizabeth Arden bed jacket. We combed her thinning hair. She sat up in bed and managed a smile. She defied the surgeons, oncologists, and endocrinologists. She defied the odds. When she felt particularly well, we took short trips together, never mentioning past or future. We packed evening clothes, climbed aboard the Delta Queen paddle wheeler, cruised downriver to New Orleans, and back home in autumn when the shores blazed like gold.

In the middle of a winter, she thought we might catch the train and spend a few days at The Greenbrier in West Virginia. In a snowstorm, she bundled in her furs and Joe Collins drove us over to the Lexington Railroad Station and loaded us onto that grand old train, The Chesapeake and Ohio. We scooted to our cozy little compartment like schoolgirls, ordered tea and cakes, and whipped out the cards. We played Gin Rummy until the porter tapped on our door and sang out, "Dinner is served in the main dining car."

In those days, dining car tables were laid with starched linens, china, crystal, and gleaming silver. We lingered over dinner, watching the lights of towns and mountain villages flash by and the sleet beating hard on our window. Back in our cocoon, we fell asleep as soon as our heads hit the pillows, as the old C & O rocked and swayed through the mountains. We arrived just as dawn was breaking, in a heavy snow. Railroad car doors were iced and the road from the hotel down to the station was impassable for the limousines that always met the train. Instead, waiting for us was a carriage drawn by two fine dark horses wearing bells on their harnesses. The driver, dressed in top hat and cape, pulled heavy wool robes around us and off we went, up and around the snowy hills in silence but for the bells and the *swish swish* of sleigh runners. The breath of the horses froze in the high clear air. We rounded a bend and far ahead the Greenbrier loomed like a glittering ice palace.

We played cards beside the enormous yule log that burned night and day. I swam for her and she applauded my water ballet. I bowled and she kept score. We went to the theatre to see Doris Day fall in love with Rock Hudson. We ate in the sunniest corner of the dining room or ordered breakfast in bed, took high tea by the fire, dressed for dinner and dined beside the string quartet. Every time we turned around, a tall gray-haired gentleman nodded and smiled at Sallie Gay, and finally sent pink (how did he know to send pink?) roses to the room with his card, asking her to dinner. He was smitten with her green eyes.

———

It was our last trip together. She died in my arms on an August afternoon while Joe Collins, Eva Belle, Sudie, and Tott waited outside. I climbed onto the hospital bed and rested her head on my shoulder. I whispered in her ear, telling her stories, until she closed her eyes for the last time. I recalled a summer day when the pony and I bit each other, my greasy hat with guinea hen feathers. I told her how deeply I loved her; of the pride I took in her courage, her smile, her passionate liberal politics, her gift to make others laugh; and how much I wanted to be like her. My beautiful mother closed her sea-green eyes.

We were both accepting, even agreeable to her dying by the time it came, but after her death there were dreams, dreams, and more dreams: of telephone calls from her to set the time and place we should meet for lunch; of mad racing to meet her at the Lafayette Hotel Grill, but I was always just one minute too late. Only Horatio Mason, who ran the Hotel garage, stepped out to meet me. "Your mother just left, you just missed her." I dreamed our home had more rooms than I had ever seen, with walls made of glass and blinding lights that blazed inside and out, casting long shadows over the lawn. She reigned there happily at her dinner table with family and friends. In another dream, I stepped out onto the back porch and came upon her arranging fresh-cut flowers in the deep sink, tossing the long green stems into a shining copper pail. Before I could catch her, she scurried down the long front hall, past the old grandfather clock, and out the front door, laughing softly.

———

Perhaps these recollections now will allow me to finally arrive in time for lunch at the Lafayette Grill, to catch up with my mother by the grandfather clock in the hallway, to walk beside her again, and out the front door.

Time never let up again. It whipped around like the second hand on Doc's *sip-sip-sip* Bulova wristwatch, and my Joe Collins died in his sleep at seventy-five. "Jesus, help me now, my sweet Joe's gone," Miss Mattie wept for all of us, as Zack and Rabbit tried to comfort her. The church was packed; they stood outside on the wide steps and lined the sidewalk down South Main Street. Little Rabbit looked a century old. He had always been frail and Joe liked to tease him, *Don't you turn sideways on me, Little Rabbit, or I can't see you.* How in the world did that spindly little man heave heavy tobacco stalks while he straddled poplar rails at the top of the barn thirty feet over the earth? "It's alright, Pig, Joe's gone on home." Rabbit's hand settled on Joe's chest and brushed as delicately as a feather over his heart. "He looks real nice, real nice. Still wearing that tie you gave him." He sucked in his breath between tobacco-stained teeth and exhaled with the finality of a last breath, maybe to recreate Joe's last act or set his own mind straight about dying, or maybe he was just bone tired from working all his life and for what? The tie looked a little careworn now, but it was still an iridescent blue-green peacock beneath Rabbit's hand. Mattie found the Christmas card, "To Joe from Pig," and gave it to me, along with the little penknife they found in my granddaddy's hand that day in the patch.

Joe's leaving wrote our last chapter in the place we called Heaven's Little Footstool, and that day I carried Joe Collins and my memories home alone: my first chew of the sweet Apple, that first moment I sat alone on ol' John Deere and eased the key in the ignition to the right. *Crank it over, Pig, he wants to run, just give him the gas!* Sure enough, the grinding of the engine led to a sputter and then a backfire you could hear in the next county. *Go easy now*, he yelled as I drove the new green and yellow machine around and around a five-acre field of cattle while he walked beside me.

My heart wanted to hear more wild tales down by the ice-cold artesian spring. *Let it fly, Pig, show these boys what you got. Don't she beat all, spitting like that?* I wanted to slip onto the soft leather seat in the truck beside him and ride out to Ocean Frog's store, or smoke our Lucky Strikes in the tack room while we worked saddle soap deep into halters and bridles. *It's time for you to take the old mules' reins.* Together we moved in silence behind Kate and Beck to the jingle of harness and the pounding of my heart beneath the overalls.

The hearse came to a halt by his open grave and I stepped onto a field of deep meadow grass. Old maple trees moved in the afternoon breeze. It was summertime, our time, and I saw him clear as day, walking away from me, dressed in those pale blue Fink's and carrying his lunch pail. It was so many years ago when he tasted a little dirt and dabbed at his mouth with the pink bandanna. *You remember when my time comes, to add Joe*

Collins to this earth, you hear me, Pig? Yes, Sir, I will. I promised him that, but I knew he would never leave me. He would always be just around a curve, over the next hill, or across the bridge to bring me home, and there he stood in the meadow running the pink bandanna over the top of his fine brown head. He threw up his hands and hollered to me, *Little Pig, I believe it's time for a taste of the sweet Apple.*

I can see Eva Belle pursing her lips, nodding her stylish gray head and saying, "They've all gone home now, all laid to rest." She had a place for everybody to go. "The weary will find their eternal rest, the tormented will find peace, bless their hearts, and the ugly-acting ones, well, they'll get hellfire and damnation, and that's just what they deserve. Lord knows, there's bound to be some justice in this tired old world." And Lord knows, my people in that cemetery greatly outnumber those living today.

I wonder, will I write my final chapter there, will my history abide in the Bluegrass? Where is home? There isn't a single shopkeeper in the little town who remembers me and only a handful recall my father's name. Grassy Springs Farm has been sold; the house that kept us since 1849 burned to the ground. A summer tornado struck two of my granddaddy's great tobacco barns, shredding them into kindling. Ocean Frog would turn in his grave if he knew his little store had been razed to make way for The Apostolic House of Prayer. Even Joe Collins' little green cottage is gone. I move through my days with the spells my people cast. I would ask them to lay me to rest where the great oaks are hollowed by summer lightning, where stone walls ease along Grassy Springs Pike, on the very spot where I took the communion of my first chew—but they've gone and torn down the barn!

ACKNOWLEDGMENTS

This book was never written with publication in mind. The first draft was purloined by two lifelong friends, and given to Dr. Jane Gentry Vance, who sent the unpunctuated, misspelled piece to Algonquin. Having taken a life of its own, *Sweet Apple* flew back home to Sarabande Books. I never dreamed they would find my stories remotely interesting... my place in time was so long ago. My parents and Joe Collins left too early, when my daughter Carla Harris and son Peter were too young; so I wrote in the hope that my grandson, Holt, who is five now, might someday read this journal and come to love Joe Collins, and understand our way of life in the Bluegrass.

I want to thank Toss and Mary Ann for stealing my book. I thank Jane Gentry—who said I was a *storyteller* at our very first meeting—and I am eternally grateful for May Wetherby Jones, my Auntie Mame, who adopted me years ago and has given me her unceasing support, encouragement, and wisdom ever since. When I turned my hand to writing, she listened to Woodford County tales as we drove the thousand miles to Naples, Florida, and again on the beach by the gulf, and yet again over the phone. Last summer Toss, Mary Ann, and I took a picnic to my mother's grave, made ourselves comfortable against her headstone, and read "The Playtex Panty Girdle" and "The Pink Tutu" aloud. I thank them for listening and I am grateful for their support. To the mysterious fates that lured me back to hunt again for guinea hen feathers under the crabapple tree with Joe Collins, I want to say, this was the happiest and most self-defining journey of my life.

I am fortunate beyond all to have had young, brilliant editors receive my unpolished stories with open arms. Thanks to Sarah Gorham and Kristina McGrath, I am learning more about the appropriate usage of paragraphs and commas. I am proud to be published by Sarabande Books and *that's* the understatement of the year!

THE AUTHOR

Jo Anna "Pee-Wee" Holt Watson was born and reared in Woodford County, Kentucky, the heart of the Bluegrass. An entrepreneur and recycling advocate, she was co-owner of Bandana Yardbird, a company that used garden tool parts to produce whimsical birdlike yard sculptures. According to *The Atlanta Constitution,* "Pee-Wee travels around the country wearing a blue blazer and a straw hat preaching the gospel of recycling." Holt Watson is a fourth-generation Kentuckian and self-proclaimed Yellow Dog Democrat. She is an amateur photographer, gardener, avid sportsperson, former horse trials judge, and creator of *Plumbline,* a series of televised panel discussions regarding critical political and social issues. She was responsible for bringing together Jane Morton Norton and John Walsh to establish the Morton Center. Jo Anna Holt Watson lives in Louisville, Kentucky, with her Airedale, Harrie Holt, and Welsh Terrier, Maggie Tarbell.

David Woods